D0850395

QUANTUM SUCCESS

Also by Christy Whitman
Taming Your Alpha Bitch
The Art of Having It All

QUANTUM SUCCESS

7 Essential Laws for a Thriving, Joyful, and
Prosperous Relationship with Work and Money

CHRISTY WHITMAN

Foreword by Lisa Nichols

ENLIVEN BOOKS
—
ATRIA

New York   London   Toronto   Sydney   New Delhi

ENLIVEN™

ATRIA

First Enliven Books hardcover edition September 2018

This publication contains the opinions and ideas of its author. It is intended to provide helpful and informative material on the subjects addressed in the publication. It is sold with the understanding that the author and publisher are not engaged in rendering medical, health, or any other kind of personal professional services in the book. The reader should consult his or her medical, health, or other competent professional before adopting any of the suggestions in this book or drawing inferences from it.

The author and publisher specifically disclaim all responsibility for any liability, loss, or risk, personal or otherwise, which is incurred as a consequence, directly or indirectly, of the use and application of any of the contents of this book.

Interior design by Amy Trombat

Manufactured in the United States of America

10 9 8 7 6 5 4 3 2 1

Library of Congress Cataloging-in-Publication Data

Names: Whitman, Christy, author.
Title: Quantum success : 7 essential laws for a thriving, joyful, and
    prosperous relationship with work and money / Christy Whitman ; foreword by Lisa Nichols.
Description: New York : Atria/Enliven Books, 2018.
Identifiers: LCCN 2018022901 (print) | LCCN 2018024564 (ebook) | ISBN
    9781501179020 (eBook) | ISBN 9781501179006 (hardback) | ISBN 9781501179013 (paperback)
Subjects: LCSH: Self-actualization (Psychology) | Success. | BISAC: SELF-HELP
    / Personal Growth / Success. | BUSINESS & ECONOMICS / Motivational. |
    SELF-HELP / Personal Growth / Happiness.
Classification: LCC BF637.S4 (ebook) | LCC BF637.S4 W4825 2018 (print) | DDC 158.1—dc23
LC record available at https://lccn.loc.gov/2018022901

ISBN 978-1-5011-7900-6
ISBN 978-1-5011-7902-0 (ebook)

Are you unintentionally blocking yourself
from creating the success you desire?

Find out by completing your own
Quantum Success personal assessment.

Go to QuantumSuccessBook.com/quiz
and enter code 7Quantum18.

To My Divine as my CEO: Thank you for guiding me toward my desires, in my business and in my life.

And to my family: Frederic, Alex, and Maxim.
I deeply appreciate and love you.

CONTENTS

Foreword by Lisa Nichols xi

Introduction 1

1: You (Alone) Are the Creator of You 9

2: Upending the Superstition of Materialism 37

3: Controlling Your Own Emotional Dial 65

4: Conjuring the Essence of Quantum Success 87

5: Living Into Your Future 109

6: Creating the Climate for Quantum Success 135

7: Pruning as a Catalyst for Growth 167

Conclusion 195

Acknowledgments 199

Endnotes 201

FOREWORD

Lisa Nichols

GROWING UP IN SOUTH CENTRAL LOS ANGELES, I faced the harsh reality of living paycheck to paycheck. And for the first twenty-eight years of my life, every action I took in relation to my career was simply to earn one more paycheck.

Getting a job was never difficult for me; I've always been a strong communicator, and therefore a good interviewer. Keeping a job once I got it, however, was a different story. I was grateful for the money I earned—and in fact had chosen accounting because it was one of the more lucrative fields available to me—but the work was rote and lacked any sense of purpose or meaning. Over time, I even grew to resent it: Why should I spend my time balancing other people's accounts when I barely had enough in my own to cover *my* monthly bills?

At twenty-nine, after getting fired from my fourth job in five years, I was sitting in the living room of my small apartment, halfheartedly scanning the classifieds while the TV droned on in the background. I'd been out of work for three months, I was a week and a half late paying my portion of the rent, and my car had just been repossessed. Yet I was still having a hard time motivating myself into action. I'd circled a handful of jobs that I knew I was qualified for, but every time I reached for the phone, I felt nauseated and unable to make the call. These were the days before I'd learned to interpret the subtle messages from my intuition, and could only hear them when they became strong enough to hit me like a proverbial sledgehammer.

Stalling, I turned my attention to the TV, where a man was telling a story about walking home from work every night and passing an elderly couple seated on their front porch, their golden retriever lying in between their two rocking chairs. The first night as the man passed, he heard the dog let out a tiny yelp. The next night as he passed by, the dog again yelped, as if in pain. On the third night as the man approached the house, the dog let out what sounded like an agonized moan. Finally, the man—perplexed by the situation—stopped and addressed the couple. "I'm sorry to bother you," he said. "But I pass by here each night on my walk home from work, and every night I've seen your dog lying in that same spot, crying out in pain. Is there something the matter with him?" The elderly woman replied, "Well, you see, honey, the dog is lying on a nail." Still confused, the man asked, "Well, if that's the case, why doesn't he just move?" The woman sighed, still rocking back and forth in her chair, and said, "It only hurts him enough to lie there and moan about it, not enough to get up and move someplace else."

Hearing this story, I realized that, just like that dog, I was stuck in a pattern of going from one unfulfilling job to the next, and while I often complained about the condition of my life, I'd never realized that I had the ability to choose to do something different. Finally I had the courage to ask myself the question that I'd long been avoiding. I went into the bathroom and looked at my reflection in the mirror as I silently asked myself, "What do I really want to do with my life?" To my surprise, the answers came effortlessly: *I want to travel the world. I want to help other people. I want to wear a black business suit, and I want to carry a laptop computer.*

From that point forward, I approached my career with a very different mind-set. Now seeking work that made my heart sing in addition to making ends meet, I interviewed each prospective company as much as they were interviewing me. Not long after, I accepted a position with a computer software manufacturer that provided all the opportunities I'd been looking for: I traveled up and down the coast of California, helping others by training them to use a new software system that would make their jobs easier. I bought myself a sharp black business suit—and, of course, being in the tech industry, I naturally carried a laptop computer! But the opportunities to contribute in meaningful ways did not end there.

In most cases, the people that I was responsible for training were completely unfamiliar with computers, and many felt intimidated or even threatened by the prospect of changing over to a new system. To help ease their anxiety and encourage them to shift into a more positive mental state, I began delivering a one-hour motivational talk before each training session. Over time, I received such rave reviews from audiences that soon I was able to delegate the software training to a colleague and focus all my energy on doing what truly lit me up—and what has ultimately become my life's work: motivating the masses. Each new opportunity unfolded as a result of embracing the one that came before—starting with that fateful day I stopped working for a paycheck and started living my purpose.

The first of many quantum leaps in my career began with a willingness to take this kind of leap, to listen to the big *yes* in my belly, to "feel the fear and do it anyway," to move forward in the direction of my heart even when mentally I had no idea where it would lead. What I now know in my bones that I did not know all those years ago is that, regardless of our circumstances, our past conditioning, or the unique challenges that have shaped each one of us, we are all being guided by divine forces that always have our back.

In this book, Christy Whitman—my soul sister and fellow spiritual warrior—shows you how, thought by thought and step by step, you can bridge the distance from the level of success you are currently experiencing in relation to your career, to embodying the full expression of all that you were born to contribute—and to receiving all the abundance that is your birthright. As a teacher and coach who's been applying the principles of deliberate creation for more than twenty years, Christy knows whereof she speaks, and with refreshing transparency she guides you through an actionable plan to create the career success you desire.

As you will soon learn from all you will discover in these pages, "quantum" success goes far beyond the amount of money we earn. In fact, if our main goal is money, we often place an unnecessary cap on the full impact we are here to make. Money has us think in shortsighted ways, and often it's not until we reach a point of complete dissatisfaction—as I did—with this one-dimensional approach that we become willing to look for the bigger reason we are here, for the bigger contribution we are here to make. When you discover how to utilize your unique talents in the service of others, a thriving career and a rich, abundant life are the natural by-products.

Lisa Nichols
Los Angeles, CA
Fall 2017

QUANTUM
SUCCESS

INTRODUCTION

THIS BOOK BEGINS WITH A PREMISE that you must accept in order to benefit from its powerful message: You and your life are unlimited. YOU are a beautiful, blessed being. The energy that animates your body, that moves the air in and out of your lungs, that arises in your mind as impulses and desires, and that is expressed through your unique interests and talents . . . the energy that flows through every aspect of your body and mind is the same energy that governs the process of all creation—whether the creation of a single cell or an entire universe. By whatever name you call it—life force, Mother Nature, Spirit, source, or God—*you* are an extension of this powerful force. You are the furthermost tangible expression of it, in fact: a divine being living in a seemingly material world.

You have arrived here, at this particular juncture in time, with all of your particular characteristics and circumstances, for the purpose of realizing your own divinity. You are here to experience the fullness of your power, to make manifest your heart's desires, and to create a magnificent life that continues to surprise and delight not just you, but everyone in your personal and professional realm.

Although you have taken form as a human being who is temporarily focusing through your unique body and this particular lifetime, you are not separate from the energy that created you, from the energy that creates worlds. You come from the same source from which all things arise, and to which all things return. You are part of the ocean of consciousness that contains everything, and you are here to allow your life's journey to guide you along a unique and winding path. And once that path has reached its fullest expression and farthest expansion, the essence of you will rise like rain evaporating back into the clouds, and the river of your life will merge into and again become one with the broader ocean.

While you are here in this lifetime, you will be called by many streams of interest, and each one of them will provide you an opportunity to flow your energy and your love. Your career is one such tributary—one that holds unlimited potential for inspiration, expansion, contribution, abundance, and, quite frankly, the most thrilling ride of your life.

Your career is a living, breathing, evolving manifestation that has the potential to contract, stagnate, wither, and die, or to grow, blossom, expand, and thrive. In the same way that a child, a lover, a pet, or even a houseplant is responsive to the quality of attention you focus upon it, this aspect of your life responds to and will reflect back to you the quality of energy you give to it. This book will guide you through each stage of this becoming—from the earliest conception of the vision in the inner world of your imagination and emotions, to its full manifestation in the external world of form and phenomenon. And once you have brought into full fruition the vision of your ideal career as you can right now conceive it, this book will show you how to periodically *re-create* that vision so that it continues to fulfill your ever-evolving desires.

Your career is a living, breathing, evolving manifestation that has the potential to contract, stagnate, wither, and die, or to grow, blossom, expand, and thrive.

Growing your career into a perfect manifestation of all that you want it to be is a process of bringing all aspects of yourself into resonance with the energy of what you want to create. You do this by first identifying the emotional, vibrational essence of who you want to be and how you want to feel in the area of your creative expression, and then by bringing your vibration—meaning the sum total of your dominant thoughts, feelings, moods, and emotions—into energetic harmony with that vision. Said another way, in order to create outrageous abundance in your career, you first have to become a vibrational match to the energy of abundance. If the energy you offer in relation to your career is one of anxiety or frustration, you will unwittingly hold apart from yourself the abundance you're seeking. In this book, I will show you how to purposefully adjust your energy so the vibration you are sending out is consistent with the success you desire. When that shift occurs, you will no longer find yourself striving for success. Rather, success—in all its forms—will pursue you.

When I was first introduced to the principles of deliberate creation nearly twenty years ago, the circumstances of my life were far from how I wanted them to be. I was thirty pounds overweight and nearly $60,000 in debt. I wanted to get married and start a family, but had a knack for consistently attracting the "wrong" kind of men. I worked at a job I hated and lived in an ant-infested room that I rented in someone else's home because I could not afford my own apartment.

Wanting very much to transform my life, which felt at the time like a constant uphill struggle, I devoted all my nights and nearly every weekend to studying the principles that I'll be sharing with you throughout this book. I learned about the nonphysical forces—such as

polarity, clarity, alignment, resonance, momentum, and magnetism—
that coalesce and join together to create and organize everything we
experience in our physical, manifested world, from the degree of health
and vitality we feel in our bodies, to the circumstances of where we live,
to the level of success we realize in all our endeavors. And then, determined to test the accuracy of all that I'd learned, I decided to apply these
principles to the conditions of my own life—and my career (or, more
accurately at the time, my lack thereof) offered the perfect environment
to conduct these experiments. I began a daily practice of meditating,
visualizing, magnetizing, and connecting with the energy of success, in
order to determine the outer effects of these internal practices.

Over the course of the next five years, I went to work for a series
of companies—and each new position I accepted offered a higher sal-
ary, more benefits, better working conditions, and greater freedom. A
couple of years into my "experiment," I decided to pursue a career as a
pharmaceutical sales representative, and eventually accepted a position
with Janssen Pharmaceutica, where I became the number-one rep in my
district. Everything I had intended was unfolding more easily and abundantly than I could possibly have imagined. And when at the peak of
this newfound success I was asked to resign from that position, I trusted
that the universe had better things in store for me, and immersed myself
even deeper in my metaphysical practices. I was beginning to understand that by holding steady to my vision and aligning with the essence
of what I wanted, I would eventually call that reality into my experience.
And that's exactly what happened.

After being asked to resign my position as a pharmaceutical sales
rep, I didn't work for more than three months, yet, amazingly, made
more money than when I was working full-time. Thanks to a generous
severance package, some unexpected bonuses, and windfalls that seemed
to come out of nowhere, hardly a day went by that I didn't receive a
check in the mail. During that three-month period, I also wrote my first
book, *Perfect Pictures*, and when it came out and I began promoting it,

the VP at the new company I'd started working for invited me to do a book signing at one of their national conferences.

I was happier than I'd been in years. I loved my coworkers and my customers, and although I was still relatively new to the field, I was entrusted with a very big territory. Soon I was making so much money in commissions that the company had to instate a policy to cap the monthly income of its sales force! After this occurred, a job recruiter I'd never hired called me offering a position that was even more ideal than the one I was in—with no caps on bonuses, a smaller and therefore more manageable territory, and a product that was easier to sell and more in line with my values.

I continued applying these universal principles, and everything in my life kept getting better and better. When statements from the Social Security Administration came in the mail that showed the dramatic increase in my income, it was incredibly empowering to see the tangible evidence of my expanding abundance. When I began my experiment, I was earning $32,000 a year. And when I decided to leave corporate America to start my own coaching practice so I could teach others all that I was learning, that number had skyrocketed to $186,000. In case you're wondering, it's grown by almost a full zero since then.

In this book, I'll share the success principles I've applied since the very beginning—first to become increasingly successful in my sales career, then to launch my coaching business, and finally to support its exponential growth. I'll walk you through the proven formula I've developed as a result of more than twenty years of studying, experimenting with, and applying the universal forces that govern all manifestation, and show you how to harness it to create or re-create a career expression that is ideal for you in every imaginable way. I'll show you how to establish an inner relationship with future clients, associates, and employees long before you ever meet them; how to work with light and energy to magnetize the opportunities and resources that will contribute to your success; and how to create a culture of value and appreciation around you that brings out the very best in everyone you come in contact with.

You were born with great purpose, and when you allow yourself to align with—rather than resist, contradict, or deny—that purpose, you thrive in every possible way. *Quantum success* is the natural consequence of this alignment. It is a state of appreciating all that we have created, even as we recognize that we are in the process of creating so much more.

> **You were born with great purpose, and when you allow yourself to align with—rather than resist, contradict, or deny—that purpose, you thrive in every possible way.**

Quantum success is not the result of hard work alone, of effort or struggle. Rather, it unfolds naturally and exponentially once we learn how to harness the power and energy of the universe. It is the kind of success that is created from the inside out. Each of us will define quantum success in our own terms, according to our own values, unique interests, and goals. But regardless of what it looks like on the outside, it is always marked by an internal experience of happiness, joy, vitality, aliveness, and unlimited abundance.

While some may regard a desire for this type of success as superficial or materialistic, success that arises from a state of inner alignment is a deeply spiritual pursuit, because the only way to attain it is by deciding to use this lifetime to realize the fullness of your divinity, your power, and your ability to create. You are in a continual process of becoming, and by consciously choosing *who you want to be* and *what you want to create* in the area of your career and self-expression, you accelerate this evolution.

No matter where you are right now—whether you're actively seeking to work your way up the corporate ladder, or you're reevaluating your current career path; whether you have aspirations that you don't yet know how to achieve, or you're the head of your own thriving business and are ready to create even more success with greater ease—the process outlined in this book will help you to determine with greater clarity what you now want to create, who you want to become in the process of creating it, and how to align yourself on every level with that vision.

If you desire to find and express the essence of who you are; if you are ready to allow yourself to move with clarity and momentum along the river that is your life; if you are eager to experience the exaltation, abundance, and joyful motion forward that is naturally produced from a state of internal alignment, this book will be your guide.

1

YOU (ALONE) ARE THE CREATOR OF YOU

"Do not wait. The time will never be 'just right.' Start where you stand, and work with whatever tools you may have at your command, and better tools will be found as you go along."

—NAPOLEON HILL

THE MOST THRIVING, SUCCESSFUL, JOYFUL, EXPANSIVE CAREER that you could ever imagine for yourself exists right now, in this moment, as a possibility that can be realized by you at any time. While it may not yet be known to you, it is a vision of you operating at your highest capacity, firing on all cylinders, living in the flow, and being fueled by a continually renewed passion for whatever you are engaged in. This vision includes not just yourself and your own personal sense of accomplishment, but encompasses also the abundance that flows into and out of your life, and the people with whom you deeply desire to share those resources. It includes not just the arena of work and career expression, but all of the things you want to build and create in your life: the personal mastery you desire, the adventures you are seeking, and all of those you desire to experience them with.

Whether you define your ideal career as starting your own business, rising to a desired position within the company you currently work for or wish to work for, or landing your very first job, the essence of this vision already exists within you, in your heart of hearts. You have been dreaming it into place, frame by frame, in response to the precise experiences your life has caused you to desire. From all the days you have worked in a job that was less than satisfying, or watched others do the same, you have drawn some very clear conclusions about the kind of vocation that would be most pleasing to you. Conclusions such as:

- I want a greater sense of freedom.

- I want to spend my time doing things I sincerely love to do.

- I want greater control over the amount of money that flows into my life.

- I want to feel the exhilaration of a new idea being born within me, and the sensation of empowerment as I run with that new idea.

- I want to attract other solid, stable, happy, productive, effective people with whom I can co-create.

For all of the days of your life, you have been dreaming about a career expression that would serve as a conduit for this degree of quantum success, and the universe has been a silent witness to that dream as it has evolved within you, thought by thought, idea by idea. And the person you will become as you allow this dream to unfold into full physical manifestation will fill you with the joy, enthusiasm, passion, and sense of aliveness that makes life worth living.

The success that you desire in your career—however you define it—vibrates at a particular frequency, and you are no stranger to this vibration. In fact, you've felt it, sensed it, and glimpsed it many times throughout your life. You've recognized this potential in yourself in those moments when you focused all of your love, all of your intention, and all of your energy toward the accomplishment of something that really mattered to you. You've seen it demonstrated in the professional athletes whose performances thrill you, and you've felt it flowing from the leaders and luminaries who have inspired humanity throughout time.

History is filled with examples of men and women who did not permit the current reality of their life experience to write the script for what came next. People who held tenaciously to what they knew in their hearts was possible—even in the face of failure, and often without a shred of evidence to support it. The greatest leaders in every field—the scientists, inventors, social reformers, activists, artists, and philosophers who are now our heroes and heroines—have all had one important characteristic in common: they gave more credence to the vision that called them than to any voice of disbelief or doubt. Here are just a few quick cases in point:

Jennifer Lopez, the Grammy Award–winning "triple threat" singer, dancer, and actress who has risen to become one of the most famous entertainers in the world and is now reported to have a net worth of more than $250 million, held tight to her vision of success even when her mother's disapproval of her choice not to go to college left her homeless at eighteen. J. K. Rowling, creator of the Harry Potter series—one of the most popular book and film franchises in history—conceived the magical fantasy world that has delighted millions of readers around the world while unemployed, on welfare, and struggling to support her young daughter after her marriage ended in divorce. During her June 2008 commencement address at Harvard University, she said, "We carry all the power we need inside ourselves already; we have the power to imagine better." Rowling's ability to focus her imagination beyond the dire circumstances in which she found herself liberated her from the shackles of depression and hopelessness and connected her to the wellspring of creativity to which each one of us has access.

Rocker Joan Jett started her own band at the age of fifteen, and, after getting rejection letters from twenty-three separate record companies, she remained undeterred. Instead of believing the naysayers, she started her own label and released her first of what would become a huge library of hit singles, including "I Love Rock 'n' Roll." Comedian Tina Fey made history by becoming the first female head writer on the iconic TV show *Saturday Night Live*. Staggering accomplishments such as these have occurred in virtually every field and every facet of life. How has this been possible? Simple. These folks had a vision, and they held fast to it, even when others discouraged them or it looked impossible to achieve.

A visionary is someone who gives more credence to the power of his or her own mind and imagination than to the apparent limitations of any present circumstance. What all great visionaries have in common is a willingness to reach beyond the status quo and to look past their own limitations. And in that reaching, they transcend what most humans have collectively defined as the boundaries of time, money, space—even gravity. Their desire calls them outside the conditions of their own minds and allows them to tap into a universal creative force much bigger than themselves. Once accessed, this force guides them in inexplicable ways toward the perfect next step in their becoming. It is exactly as Henry David Thoreau described in this—one of his most famous quotations—and one that I have been reciting out loud for years:

"If one advances confidently in the direction of his dreams, and endeavors to live the life which he has imagined, he will meet with a success unexpected in common hours. He will put some things

behind, will pass an invisible boundary; new, universal, and more liberal laws will begin to establish themselves around and within him; or the old laws be expanded, and interpreted in his favor in a more liberal sense, and he will live with the license of a higher order of beings."

The "common hour" thinking that Thoreau writes about refers to the very common—and very detrimental—human tendency to allow the conditions in which we find ourselves to determine what we do, what we believe we can accomplish, and how we feel. Posing as the truth, these considerations come camouflaged as legitimate concerns that go something like this: *I don't have the money. It's not the right time. What will others think? If I go for my dream, I might fail. I should just be happy with the life I have.* Any thought or belief that points out man-made limits within a human experience that is, in fact, unlimited can be counted as common-hour thinking—along with any phrase that begins with the words *I can't.*

These common-hour concerns appear as formidable external conditions over which we are powerless, but this is both an illusion and a critical error in thinking. The obstacle that stands in our way is not a money problem or a time problem; it's a *thinking* problem. When our thinking is aligned with and assembled around the current conditions of our lives, we deprive ourselves of access to our innate ability to create anything different. But by applying the Law of Deliberate Creation—which is based on the understanding that what we direct our energy toward, we begin to attract—we reclaim the power to create each aspect of our lives on purpose rather than by default.

Right now in your own life, you are surrounded by conditions and considerations that may have you convinced that you are powerless to reach the next level of success that you desire in your career. You may believe you're too old, that your ideas are nothing special, or that everything you desire to accomplish has already been done before. However these thoughts, beliefs, and perceptions show up for you, it's imperative that you begin to recognize them for what they really are. They are not the truth, but you will make them your truth if you continue to affirm them.

There Is No Such Thing as a "Do-Over"

Some people believe that in order to conceive a vision for what they now want to create in any aspect of life requires a clear heart and a blank slate. But this isn't the way life works. Sometimes our expectations are not met; we run into obstacles we never anticipated, or fall short of an important goal despite giving it our very best effort. In times like these, it's so easy to fall into despair or self-judgment. And it's also easy to believe that we need to somehow right the wrongs that have been done by ourselves and others—but not only is this like marching in the opposite direction of what is wanted, it's not even possible. Every step we take— even those that feel backward—has helped us to arrive at the desires we hold today. In the same way that Thomas Edison described inventing the lightbulb not as having failed more than nine hundred times but as a process that required a thousand important steps, each setback that we live through gives us incredible clarity about the new direction we now want to take. The contrast of living what we don't want is as essential to the creative process as holding a clear vision of what we do.

> Each setback that we live through gives us incredible clarity about the new direction we now want to take.

Everything that comes into being in this manifested universe—from the birth of a baby to the start of a revolution—arises from the interplay of opposite values: dark and light; emptiness and fullness; desire and satiation; expansion and contraction. The experience of *not* realizing an important goal; of *not* being where you want to be in your career; of *not* feeling satisfied with what you are doing or *not* knowing what is next for you—all these are vitally important stepping-stones toward what is wanted. In the same way that the tide cannot rise again until it has fully receded, there can be no satisfaction without having first experienced hunger. There is an ebb and flow in all of life, and periods of not enjoying what you are doing and uncertainty about what's next are essential to the clarity that will eventually come forth as a result. While uncomfortable, pain is actually one of our greatest motivators. When our dissatisfaction with the status quo has reached a climax and we are no longer willing or able to continue down the same path, our discomfort forces open a door that allows a new range of experiences to enter our lives. The important distinction, however, is to understand pain as a force that is motivating us to a brighter future, not as an excuse to beat ourselves up for choices made or not made in the past.

Three Thousand Knives

Without the understanding that our career expression must, by necessity, include times of ebb as well as flow, we can easily slip into patterns of self-doubt, distrust, or blame when a project doesn't turn out as we had hoped. Finding ourselves smack-dab in the middle of one of life's ebbs when we desperately wanted or needed the flow can activate our lowest thoughts and darkest beliefs about ourselves and about life. But to dwell in the energy of doubt or regret has the same effect on the creative process that stabbing yourself with three thousand knives would have on your health. In a state of self-recrimination, we are blinded to resources, opportunities, and solutions that may be right in front of us, and unable to reap the benefits of our own actions. Throughout this book we will explore exactly how that is so and what to do about it; but for now, I ask you simply to soften into the possibility that we are all always arriving at a new beginning. This is true whether you've just pulled off a huge victory or are looking squarely in the eyes of defeat. No matter where you are along the spectrum from empowerment to despair, the next step toward what your heart desires is always available to you.

We cannot begin any journey from any starting place other than where we are; therefore, creating a vision for the future must begin with an acknowledgment of what is so, right now. You are the age you are. You have the education and the background that you do. You have whatever degree of awareness you possess about the type of career expression you now desire, and in seeking to manifest that, you have had experiences of both success and disappointment. There is nothing that can be done about any of that, but this does not mean you are without choice. You have the power to choose whether to regard everything that currently "is" about your career from the standpoint that something has gone wrong or that you are in some way lacking, or from the perspective that it is perfect as it is, and completely enough, even though it is in a constant state of evolving.

> **You have the power to choose whether to regard everything that currently "is" about your career from the perspective that it is perfect as it is, and completely enough, even though it is in a constant state of evolving.**

From Wherever You Are Right Now

Creating your ideal career is a process of realization that occurs in incremental steps, which means it probably won't come about as the result of a dramatic quantum leap in consciousness, nor is it likely that the next evolution of your career will keep you happy forevermore. Because you are a continually growing and expanding human being, you will continue to create and re-create not just who you are in your career, but who you are in every facet of your life. Everything in this life is open-ended. There is no finish line, no ideal target that once hit will satisfy you forever. The moment we convince ourselves that there is some final destination that we must reach in order to find fulfillment, we rob our creations of the life breath they need to expand. Your ideal career expression is always in a gradual process of becoming; all you need to focus on is taking the next logical step forward from wherever you are right now. Mary Morrissey, my friend and incredible mentor, shares her story in her own words below as a powerful case in point:

I grew up near Portland, Oregon. I came from a great family, and was raised by parents who were deeply in love the entire sixty-three years they were to-gether. I had a high school experience like most young girls dream about. I was class vice president and a member of the drill team, had a lead in the junior play, and was a homecoming princess. From the time I was a little girl, I was very clear about what I wanted to be when I grew up—a teacher—and I envisioned putting all of the practical experience I was learning in high school to good use when I became a teacher myself.

Toward the end of my junior year of high school, my high school sweet-heart returned from college for spring break and, shortly thereafter, I dis-covered I was pregnant. My mother wept for me as if I had died. In her mind, all her dreams for me were dying. My family hastily threw together a ten-person wedding, and—once married—I did my best to go back to my life as usual.

One day near the end of the school year, the principal's voice boomed over the intercom, and I heard my name being called, instructing me to proceed to his office. When I arrived, the principal asked me if the "rumors" were true. To this question I responded, "Well, if the rumors you've heard are that I am preg-nant and married—in that order—then, yes." He shook his head, remarking that although I had exceptional grades and great honors, that there was no way he could permit me to return to school for my senior year. He explained that it would be completely inappropriate for a pregnant girl to get "mixed in" with the "normal" girls. This was 1966.

The principal then told me that there was a place for "people like me" to attend and complete their schooling. It was not held during daylight hours. Classes were held in the evening, and the school was in a part of Portland I had not even been allowed to drive in after dark. He told me that this was where the pregnant girls and the delinquent boys went to high school.

As news of my pregnancy spread through my small community, my once-perfect life received another sharp blow: the parents of the tight-knit group of girlfriends I had known since fifth grade forbade their daughters to have anything to do with me—as though pregnancy were somehow contagious.

Despite all of these setbacks, I continued to put one foot in front of the other in pursuit of my diploma, knowing this was the first of many credentials I would need to fulfill my dream of being a teacher.

One evening the following fall, I parked my car in a section of Portland I barely knew, and walked up the big staircase to my new "evening" high school. I remember thinking, Every girl here is pregnant or has a baby and every boy is some kind of a delinquent. THIS is my new student body.

A few months later, I welcomed my son into the world, and the following May I finally graduated from Washington Evening High School. But just as life began to get back on track, things took another major downward turn.

The July following my graduation, I found myself in an intensive care ward of a Portland hospital, where I had just been diagnosed with fatal kidney disease. One of my kidneys was completely destroyed by nephritis; the other was already 50 percent destroyed and had active nephritis. My doctors told me that my bloodstream was growing more toxic by the day, and that my only chance at survival was a surgery to remove the destroyed kidney—a surgery I could have only if they managed to reduce the toxin level in my blood enough so I could survive it. In 1967, before dialysis and transplants, my condition was a death sentence. Every doctor who examined me agreed that IF we could get that one kidney removed, I had, at most, six months to live. Finally, the

levels of toxins in my blood dropped enough for the doctors to decide to per-
form the surgery on me.

My husband and baby were staying with my parents during this time so
my mom and dad could help with our little seven-month-old son. Meanwhile,
I lay terrified and desperately alone in my hospital bed. Although I had at-
tended church growing up, the God of my upbringing was not a friendly place
to go when you felt like you had really screwed up, so the thought of praying
to God was of no comfort. I actually believed I was being punished for being
a "bad girl." The devastation of realizing that I would never be able to raise
my son, become a teacher, or live the life I so badly wanted to live was utterly
overwhelming.

The night before the surgery was scheduled, at about 10 p.m., a woman
walked into my hospital room and identified herself as a volunteer chaplain
who had come to pray with anyone having surgery the next day. This woman
had a list of the most risky and dangerous surgeries on the next day's schedule,
and she told me that my name was on the top of the list. Hearing that, reluc-
tantly I agreed to let her pray with me.

The chaplain pulled a chair up next to my bedside, but didn't do anything
that resembled prayer to me.

Instead, she asked me if I would be willing to share with her what
had been going on in my life for the past year or two. Sobbing, I told her
everything—getting pregnant, being expelled from school, losing all of my clos-
est friends, disappointing my parents, and the devastation of realizing I would
never be able to raise my son or become a teacher. When I finally stopped
talking, the woman looked at me with incredible compassion and said only,
"Mary, everything is created twice."

I had no idea what this meant; I hadn't yet gained the spiritual awareness
to even begin to understand it. When I looked confused by her statement, she
looked at me and said, "You already know this—in fact, EVERYONE knows
this and almost NO ONE knows the POWER of knowing this." She then
went on, "The sheet covering you, the bed you are lying on, the nightgown
you're wearing, the blanket, the ceiling, the walls, the floor, and all of the ma-

chines you are connected to—each one first had to begin as a thought before it could ever become a 'thing.'"

And then she said again, "Mary, you know this, you just don't know the power of knowing this."

She continued, "Mary, I hear how much you love your little boy, and I also hear how much you've been hating yourself. You feel like you've shamed yourself, you've shamed your school, you've shamed your family. And now that you're considering that everything is created twice, could you consider that there could be a correlation between those toxic thoughts and the toxicity that is ravaging your body and threatening your very life?"

The woman then suggested that through prayer, we could effect a change in what was going on in my mental, emotional, and physical systems; that prayer could affect the frequency of my thoughts in such a way that it could create a shift in my physical body; and that in the morning, possibly, when the doctors came to get me for surgery, they would notice how much better I looked, and question whether I still needed the surgery after all. The woman looked at me and asked, "Could you believe that this is possible?"

I told her the truth. "No."

The truth was, there wasn't one part of me, at this time, that could believe that she was going to say a few words and I would have some kind of miraculous healing.

The chaplain then said, "Okay. If you can't believe that, then for a moment I want you to think about how big the universe is—and that's just the known universe—and just how many possibilities are contained within it. Could you consider that in the infinite sea of possibilities we live in, that through the power of prayer and the power of shifting what is going on—not just in your physical body, but also in your mental and emotional bodies, your whole being—that we could scoop up out of your body everything that is toxic and place it in the one kidney that is going to get removed? And that when they remove that one kidney, instead of getting worse, you will get better? Could you believe that is possible?"

I didn't really think this could be a possibility, but I was moved by how deeply this woman believed that it was. Until this encounter, not one doctor or specialist had offered me even one possibility of how I could get well. And so I said, "Well, I don't know if it's probable, but maybe it's possible."

The chaplain latched on to this: "That's all we need," she said excitedly, "just one corner of your mind open to the possibility. Let's work with that." She then explained to me that the human mind is like a rubber band, and because my mind would naturally be distracted by the pain following the surgery, it would be an excellent time to stretch it.

The woman then said a prayer, during which she offered a series of what I would later understand to be "scaffolding imagery" as a way to introduce me to a new way of thinking. She guided me to imagine all the toxicity in my body being gathered and placed in the kidney that was soon to be removed:

"Mary, after the pain of surgery subsides, your mind will once again want to travel down the well-worn paths of self-loathing and shame. Whenever you find yourself thinking a self-loathing thought, immediately interrupt that thought and simply say, 'No! That left with the kidney!'

"And then, immediately imagine holding your little boy's hand, feeling the warmth of his skin, as you're walking him into his first day of kindergarten. You see a happy teacher at the door smiling at your little boy, and he is smiling, and here you are, alive and well and helping your little boy get into his first day of school.

"And as you leave your son with his teacher and walk farther into the school, you can hear the click, click, click of your heels as you round the corner, and there is YOUR classroom and you are now a teacher with a class of your own.

"And now, fast-forward in your mind many years later. You are sitting in a large stadium with hundreds of young men and women wearing caps and gowns. This is your son's high school graduation! You hear his name being called over a loudspeaker. He receives his diploma and turns to beam a beautiful smile at you. You feel the pride and happiness bursting forth from you at being able to be here with him on this special day. And you feel how proud you are for the part you've played in his growth and for how your teaching career *has grown. And now, fast-forward again. This time you are sitting in the front row at a wedding. You are the mother of the groom, and your son is marrying the love of his life. And your career as a teacher is flourishing.*

"Every time you find yourself thinking a self-loathing thought, say to yourself, 'No, that left with the kidney,' and then immediately replay all three of these images and feel them to be true. Mentally review the day you walk your five-year-old son to kindergarten, the day of his graduation from high school, and the day you are attending his wedding, knowing that during each stage of your son's growth, your teaching career has been growing just as beautifully."

The next day, I underwent the surgery as planned. The doctors removed the toxic kidney and reaffirmed that I still, in fact, had active nephritis in half of my remaining kidney. Over the next couple of weeks, my numbers stabilized, and the doctors told me I might have a little more time to live than they had initially thought. Since the numbers were stable for the time being, they let me go home to my parents' house to be cared for there. I was so sick that they sent me home in an ambulance, and I was required to be in the specialist's office three to four times a week for tests and monitoring.

Four or five months after the surgery, I was sitting in a meeting with my surgeon, the kidney specialist, and the general practitioner, and they were all scratching their heads.

"We have no medical science for why your one kidney is now functioning as a whole and perfect kidney. We will have to simply put 'medical anomaly' on your chart. But whatever you are doing, keep doing it."

And that's what I did, although I had no idea of the power of repeating the three "scaffolding" images of my life unfolding raising a healthy son and growing a teaching career.

I went on to earn my undergraduate degree in education, then attended a two-year seminary, following that with a master's degree in counseling psychology, as well as an honorary doctorate in humane letters.

Exactly five years after the volunteer chaplain had suggested it, and I had accepted it as a possibility, I found myself walking hand-in-hand with my son as I escorted him to his first day of kindergarten. I distinctly remember the click, click, click my heels made on the ground as I walked past his classroom and into my own.

Both before and after the surgery, my only definition of a "teacher" was someone who taught in a traditional K-through-12 school, but that vision evolved dramatically over the years that followed. I certainly had no way of knowing when I was lying in my hospital bed at the age of eighteen that I would go on to become a teacher of transformation to tens of thousands of people all around the world. I did not need to know that. I simply took one step and then another—first to become a traditional elementary school teacher; and then, wanting to understand how I had shifted my mind-set in such a powerful way, to become a student and teacher of spirituality and transformation.

Over time, I knew I wanted to dedicate my life to helping people manifest their dreams as well, and sometimes against seemingly overwhelming odds. I learned there is not only an art but a science to bringing dreams out of the realm of imagination and into the world of reality. And that is precisely what I have been doing for the last thirty-five years.

Mary's transformation, which she shared with me recently in a personal interview, is a perfect demonstration of the power of holding a vision. The chaplain who facilitated this shift clearly understood some of the principles and practices that I'll show you throughout this book. First, she suggested the possibility that Mary could expand her mind and create an entirely different reality than the one she was currently living out. Next, she encouraged Mary to release the negative energy she had internalized after those closest to her judged and ostracized her, and to then visualize that energy leaving her body as the doctors removed her kidney. And finally, the chaplain provided powerful, emotionally charged imagery to help Mary make that vision bold and bright, and to establish an energetic connection with the future she so dearly desired.

As you will learn in the chapters that follow, when we achieve this type of visceral relationship to our desired future, we begin to powerfully magnetize that future into our lives. And perhaps most important of all, although the woman who attended Mary that night may have sensed that her life was going to be used to serve more people than the elementary students Mary sought to reach, she did not ask Mary to visualize any of the specifics about where she would receive her training or to consider what subjects she would ultimately like to teach. Instead, in the infancy of Mary's unfolding dream, she purposefully kept the details general, having Mary focus only on the next logical steps to the life she desired: that of enjoying a thriving career as a teacher while participating in the joyful life of her child. While in the beginning she had no way of conceiving of the type of teacher she would ultimately become, the details that she *could* envision—such as teaching elementary school and attending her son's wedding—became Mary's focal point, her true north. She needed only to follow them, choice by choice, to bring into reality a dream bigger than anything Mary dared to imagine for herself.

I share this story because it is a remarkable example of how it is not necessary (or even possible) to decide right now what your endgame vision is for your career, or for any aspect of your life, for that matter. In fact, it's actually counterproductive to try to envision the most complete manifestation of your career expression, because from the vantage point of where you're now standing, it's not even within your field of vision. The day I knew I needed to quit my lucrative job in corporate America in order to follow my heart and become a coach, I could never have imagined how far down the Yellow Brick Road that single choice would take me—and you don't need to know this about your future, either.

You simply cannot, in this moment, envision the ultimate summit you will reach at the height of your career. But, like Mary, what you *can* discover in every moment is the path that feels the best to you right now, the choice that will give you a greater sense of freedom, fulfillment, clarity, and empowerment. If you are open to discovering them, you will see that your life up until this point has been offering you plenty of clues. One great way to uncover these clues is to reflect on the roles and activities that you already know you dislike doing, and to use this information to better distinguish the types of things that you *do* enjoy.

For example, I have never enjoyed working with numbers, so I knew early on that I wasn't interested in becoming an accountant or a bookkeeper, or working in the world of finance. This distinction helped me to realize that I was not a numbers gal, but a people person. Looking back, I could see that the times in my life when I felt the happiest were when I was helping people. My career as a pharmaceutical sales trainer came with plenty of baggage in the form of competition and office politics, but because I loved that the job afforded me the opportunity to help the sales team become more productive, I was successful in that role. Years later, when that job was no longer fulfilling, I sought to discover what I'd enjoy doing more, and realized that I wanted to support people in succeeding in all aspects of their lives, not just in their careers. This desire, combined with my curiosity about human potential and my commitment to continually growing and evolving as an individual, led me to becoming a coach, which was the next piece of the puzzle in what is now a fantastically rewarding career.

At this point in the process, you need only a subtle inkling of what you might enjoy doing and what skills and insights you would most like to contribute. The farther you follow that inner calling, the more specific and refined that vision will become for you.

At this point in the process, you need only a subtle inkling of what you might enjoy doing and what skills and insights you would most like to contribute.

CONNECTING TO YOUR BROADER VISION

Begin this exercise with the understanding that you are not seeking to discover the end-all, be-all vision for your career expression that will fulfill you forevermore, but simply a broad-strokes picture of the type of work you are generally good at and would enjoy doing. With that premise in mind, approach it in a soft, easy, general way. Allow whatever information arises, and in whatever level of detail, knowing that it will flesh out over time.

Reflect back over your life, noticing the high points, the peak experiences, that easily jump out at you. In which periods of your life did you feel the most inspired, or the most connected to your innate strengths and talents? When did you feel that you were making the biggest contribution to those around you? Perhaps it was when you were heavily involved in sports, or when you were a new parent, or maybe you can recall a job you had when you were younger that—while perhaps not the best career choice—was genuinely enjoyable to you.

Next, mentally place yourself back in those situations and see if you can identify what it was about these experiences that you enjoyed the most. Did they call you to show up in a way that left you feeling proud about your accomplishments? Did you feel like you were investing your energy toward contributing to an important goal? To the extent that you are able, identify the inner qualities that these situations brought to life within you, and write them down. Even if in this moment you can't make any logical correlation between these inner qualities and how they could be used in a career setting, identify them nonetheless. They represent in seed form the unique contribution that you alone are here to make. In the chapters that follow, I will show you how—with proper nourishment, and under the right conditions—they will blossom into the fullness of your magnificence and brilliance.

In the same way that Mary always dreamed of becoming a teacher and I knew from the time I was introduced to life coaching that it was a path I wanted to pursue, you have also been gathering data and coming to conclusions about the type of work that lights you up and makes the most of your natural resources and abilities. If you lean in this direction, day by day and moment by moment, you will soon find yourself living a reality that you can't even conceive of right now. Rather than trying to navigate to a destination that has not yet revealed itself to you in its entirety, focus on making choices that are based on the view you are able to see right now. To paraphrase the advice of Dr. Martin Luther King Jr., "You don't have to see the whole staircase, just take the first step."[1] And creating specific, measurable goals will help you to clarity, quantify, and define each of the steps you must take.

You don't have to see the whole staircase, just take the first step.

Breaking Down the Vision

By its very definition, a vision depicts a reality that is much bigger than the one you are currently living. In identifying it, you now have a general idea of the experiences you desire to create in each important aspect of your life, and the general feelings you believe will accompany those experiences. Remember, the act of receiving any new vision is a spiritual occurrence. It is an expression of the unmanifested aspect of you beckoning the aspect of you that exists in physical form in order to evolve you into the very best version of yourself that you can be. Once you clarify your general vision, it's important to continue to make it more actionable—and therefore more attainable—by breaking it down into specifics.

As an example, at the time I had clarified for myself that I no longer wanted to work at my corporate job, the only vision that I had formulated of my ideal career was one in which I felt free and abundant. Although I could not yet articulate any of the specifics, I knew that I wanted to work when I was inspired to work; that I wanted to be my own boss; that I wanted to exercise whenever I wanted and, in general, have the freedom to schedule my own time. I also knew that I wanted a career that would allow me to be a stay-at-home mom. Now, this description is still relatively vague, but it's heading in the right direction.

As I continued to refine this vision and make it more specific, I envisioned myself sitting at my computer happily working, knowing that my baby was being cared for in the next room and that I could see him and spend time with him whenever I wanted. I saw myself with my baby boy in my arms, walking out to the mailbox where I would collect dozens of hefty checks.

With these more detailed visions now firmly anchored in my mind, the next step was to set specific goals that would support their unfolding. So, for example, when I first conceived the vision of becoming a *New York Times* best-selling author, I spent a lot of time envisioning how I would feel to have accomplished this, and what it would do for my new career. But equally important was creating actionable goals that I knew would be involved in attaining it—such as the number of books I wanted to sell, the strategies I would use to sell them, and the resources I would need in order to implement those strategies.

If a vision provides a general sense of where you want to go, how you want to spend your time, who you want to be, and how you want to feel when you get there, then goals are like the signposts that let you know at each step along the way if you are headed in the right direction. The key to successfully achieving even a big vision lies in setting smaller goals that are perfectly aligned with it, and—as you reach each of these smaller goals—continuing to set new ones in their place.

The words *goal* and *vision* are often used interchangeably, but in reality they involve two very different processes. If you think of your vision as your desire to align yourself with the ultimate result of quantum success that you want to create, goals enable you to organize your efforts toward that vision. In taking the specific actions to achieve each of your goals, you are creating a powerful momentum in the direction of what you desire. In other words, a goal is a vision that's been broken down into increments.

One of the most effective goal-setting strategies I've ever come across is thought to have evolved from the concept of "management by objectives," which business consultant Peter Drucker wrote about in his 1954 classic *The Practice of Management.*[2] This approach to goal-setting is easy to remember, because it's organized around the acronym SMART—meaning goals are *specific, measurable, attainable, relevant,* and *time-bound.* If you make sure the goals you set for yourself are in alignment with these five characteristics, you will dramatically increase your chances of reaching them. By breaking down the components of each word, it's easy to see how each step helps to turn vague resolutions into clear, actionable steps for bringing your vision into reality.

Step 1: Set goals that are specific, meaning that anyone reading them will know exactly what it is you desire to achieve. To make your goal specific, you can ask yourself questions such as "What exactly do I want to create?" "Where do I want this to take place?" "Who do I want to create this with?" Notice the difference in intention between the goal *I want to earn more money* and the goal *I am proudly earning $20,000 per month working from home as a life coach.* The more clearly you define what it is you're reaching toward, the more energy and resources you will summon toward it.

Toward the end of 2014, about six months before my last book, *The Art of Having It All: A Woman's Guide to Unlimited Abundance,* was released, I set a very specific goal that the book would hit the *New York Times* best-seller list the week it came out. I had already had one best-selling book, which I cowrote with another author, and it was important to me to reach this milestone again with my next book. The book's exact release date was February 25, 2015, so the target and the timeline were crystal. Assigning dates to your goals, by the way, is a sure-fire way to make sure they meet the criterion of being specific.

Step 2: Set goals that are measurable, meaning that you are clear about exactly what you want to see, hear, feel, and experience once your goal is attained. A goal such as *I want to eat healthy* is one-dimensional, but the goal *I eat at least two servings each of protein and vegetables every day* defines exactly what healthy eating means to you.

In the case of my goal to become a second-time best-selling author, it was measurable in the sense that I would either make it on the *New York Times* list or I wouldn't, and either way, that fact would be easily observable. But another aspect of making a goal measurable involves breaking it down into each of the steps that need to take place from point A to point B in order to become accountable for taking each one. I did this by finding out the approximate number of books that needed to sell for a title to be considered for the list. I also spoke with one of my colleagues, another best-selling author, and found out the steps she took to achieve this status when her book was released. She educated me on the fact that the *New York Times* does not consider only the number of books that are sold, nor do they include books that are sold only through Amazon. In taking the steps to make sure my goal was mea-surable, I learned about an entire process that takes place behind the scenes in order for a book to hit the *New York Times* list, and applying this process not only helped me to reach that specific goal related to my book, but also increased my presence on the Internet and landed me all kinds of other media exposure.

Step 3: Set goals that are attainable. To do this, you will need to consider whether you have the time, money, energy, and other resources required to bring it all the way across the finish line. Another critical part of set-ting a goal that is attainable is making sure that it is something you actually have the power to accomplish. For example, *My husband is earning $100,000 per year* is not within your sphere of influence. To make it attainable, you would have to rephrase it so that it's something that you have the direct ability to create. Attainable goals are those that you alone have the power to fulfill and that do not depend on the participation or cooperation of anyone else.

In seeking to make a goal attainable, you have to know not only the precise steps involved in achieving it, but also the ins and outs—as well as the potential obstacles or pitfalls—of whatever strategy you are using so you can navigate around these or make changes as needed. A couple of months before my last book was released, for example, I was told that the *New York Times* would not consider adding a book to its best-seller list that was either self-published or published by an individual other than the author. *The Art of Having It All* was under contract to be published by Jacquie Jordan Publishing, a subsidiary of TVGuestpert, but once we uncovered this potential obstacle, we changed the copyright to read *TVG Publishing* in order to make sure this technicality would not stop it from getting on the list. When making sure your goal is attainable, you want to chart its trajectory from start to finish and make sure that nothing is likely to derail that forward momentum.

Step 4: Set goals that are relevant. It's important to direct your creative energy into outcomes that you believe will truly thrill you once you achieve them. Relevant goals are those that are in direct alignment with your vision and that light you up to think about. An easy way to find out if your goal is relevant is to ask yourself questions such as "Why do I want to create this?" "What is the objective behind the goal?" and "How do I think I will feel once I achieve it?" Something like *I want to start my own business* is a very general goal. To make it relevant, you need to clarify what attaining it would mean to you personally. *Selling handmade jewelry will allow me to earn money while engaging in my favorite hobby* is relevant, because it is connected to the underlying *why*—and as Viktor

Frankl noted, quoting Nietzsche, "He who has a *why* to live for can bear with almost any *how*."

My goal to have *The Art of Having It All* hit the *New York Times* best-seller list was absolutely relevant to my bigger vision, in the sense that the *why* behind everything I do is to assist as many people as I can—through my books, programs, and coaching methodology—to discover that they are unlimited, and so is their potential to create whatever they desire in this lifetime. The more books I sell and the more media appearances I do, the more people are exposed to my work and the more credibility I gain, not just in the self-help world but also in the eyes of everyday people who might not consider themselves spiritual or on any path of personal development.

Step 5: The final step in setting SMART goals is making sure that they are time-bound, meaning that it's not only clear what you will accomplish, but by when. My goal of becoming a second-time *New York Times* best-selling author was timely in that there was a certain period during which the books had to be sold, media appearances done, and other efforts carried out.

Making sure your goal is time-bound may require a bit of flexibility and finesse, because while timelines and deadlines do summon energy that motivate some people into action, they can actually have a reverse effect on others. If attaching a timeline to your goal inspires you or causes you to focus with more clarity or creativity, then by all means, include this step. But if you feel pressured or limited by this step, skip it. This is not a one-size-fits-all approach; by feeling your way through each step, you can tailor this process to provide the most benefit for you.

Setting goals is so important, because the more success you attract in your career and the more abundant you become, the more choices and opportunities will naturally unfold in front of you. Having clearly defined goals that keep you on track toward the fulfillment of your larger vision will ensure that you're really investing your energy where it counts and are not tempted to reach for the next shiny new opportunity. And for the same reason, it's also important to write your goals down, not just ponder them in your head. To this day, I still write out my vision and my goals at the start of every new year—a ritual I incorporated many years ago. For example, in 2008, when I launched the first coach certification course I ever offered through my Quantum Success Coaching Academy, I set a goal of teaching a total of fifty students—twenty-five in the morning class and twenty-five in the evening—and something remarkable happened the moment I committed myself to this vision. The simple act of creating this goal not only began to influence the actions I took (for example, I started teaching classes at the Learning Annex by way of introducing people to my work), but also forced me to reevaluate the way I thought about my services and to get even clearer about the value they provide. Why—in light of all the coaching programs available—would someone choose to become certified by me? What was my unique niche, and what could my philosophy and approach provide for those who fell within it? This next-level thinking about my brand produced all kinds of ideas, and brought to light opportunities that had always been there, but were only revealed to me once I started asking the right questions.

I realize that the process of goal-setting has been talked about in countless personal and professional development books; that doesn't diminish the importance of making this ritual an ongoing part of your life. Of course, some goals will naturally need to be modified as you go along, and some will ultimately take up residence on the back burner as new priorities come into view, but this ritual provides a valuable focus for the future and is an integral part of clarifying your vision.

Once you've identified—from whatever you can see from where you stand right now—a clear vision of the career expression that you want to unfold and the specific SMART goals that will mark your progress toward the fulfillment of that vision, the next step is to nourish the full blossoming of your vision from seed form to its most expanded manifestation. And like every act of creation, this process occurs from the inside out.

You (Alone) Are the Creator of You: Putting It into Action

From the platform of truly acknowledging and appreciating all of your unique talents and skills, and all that they have allowed you to create in your life already, begin to formulate a general vision of who you want to be, what you want to create, and how you want to feel in the area of your career, self-expression, and contribution. Write out your responses to the following questions:

- From where you are standing right now, what do you see that you most want to give and receive?

- How do you want to show up in relation to the work you do and the people you serve?

- What type of work environment do you most enjoy because it brings out the very best in you?

Now, as this broad-view vision of your ideal career comes into clearer focus, see if you can break it down into a few more specific images of you experiencing this new reality. If what you desire is a career that allows you to perform or teach or speak all around the world, see yourself arriving in each new locale, feeling the environment that surrounds you, connecting with the people, making a difference, being abundantly compensated for your energy, and feeling absolutely amazing in the process.

In a certification program I led several years ago, I was coaching one woman, Lola, from the stage about how to achieve this exact step.

I asked her to share her vision of her ideal career and to be as specific as she could. "I am speaking all over the world," she replied. I explained to the group that in order to engage the power of the mind, which thinks—and therefore attracts—through pictures and images, we have to make those images as detailed as possible. Within a few minutes, Lola was able to identify a specific place she has always wanted to visit (Greece), and a specific location (the Parthenon) where she could envision herself taking the stage.

Just as I coached Lola to do, give yourself permission to think broadly, and as the vision of your ideal career starts to come into view, begin to identify each of the smaller steps that will serve as specific, measurable, attainable, relevant, and time-bound goals to mark your progress as you bring this vision into being:

- What would that look like on a day-to-day basis?

- How many hours would you work?

- What kinds of activities would you do?

- Are other people present or do you work primarily alone?

The more color and dimension you can give to the vision of already being engaged in your ideal career, and the more real you can make the feeling, the more energy you will summon toward its full, real-life unfolding.

Note: Please visit christywhitman.com/QSbook to download free guided meditations that will make it even easier for you to apply these principles in your life.

2

UPENDING THE SUPERSTITION
OF MATERIALISM

"Spiritual energy flows in and produces effects . . . within the phe-
nomenal world."

—WILLIAM JAMES

THE INFORMATION THAT FOLLOWS HAS THE POWER to usher you
into an entirely new way of relating, not just to your career, but to every
other aspect of yourself and your life as well. In this chapter, I seek to
bring into the light of our current awareness some of the very outdated
perceptions we hold about ourselves, the universe in which we live, and
life in general. These worldviews, if allowed to persist, will prevent you
not only from creating a flourishing career, but from coming to know
yourself as the powerful creator you were born to be.

We live in an age when science and modern physics have proven
beyond a shadow of a doubt that everything that appears material and
static is actually made up of an ever-moving sea of energy—including
the flesh, bones, and molecules of our own physical bodies—yet most of

us still do not see ourselves through this expansive lens. Instead, we relate to ourselves and to everything around us through a worldview that Deepak Chopra, in his 2009 book *Reinventing the Body, Resurrecting the Soul,* has brilliantly termed "the superstition of materialism."[3] Deepak explains the essence of this phrase, saying, "The essential nature of the material world is not material. The essential nature of the physical world is not physical. The essential stuff of the universe is non-stuff." So too, in the same way that nearly five hundred years ago Nicolaus Copernicus upended the ridiculous notion that the world is flat, we must overturn some of the grossly outdated notions about ourselves and the universe in which we live, for these are standing squarely in our way of knowing our full creative power and living the joyful experience we all sense is possible within our hearts. Until we dismantle these limiting mind-sets, we will continue to navigate our lives according to a map that is now entirely obsolete.

> The essential nature of the material world is not material. The essential nature of the physical world is not physical. The essential stuff of the universe is non-stuff.

Dispelling the "Old-World" Map of Reality

What follows are some of the most familiar landmarks on a map of an outdated paradigm of life that I am going to affectionately refer to as "the old world." As you read these statements that reflect our most widespread mind-sets and beliefs, allow yourself to see all the ways these have seeped into the fabric of our culture, and how they have embedded themselves, in fact, into our very definition of what it is to be human. And be aware, too, that to the degree you are still subscribing—even in the most subtle and unconscious of ways—to these limitations, they will continue to hold you back, not only from the career success you desire and deserve, but from knowing yourself as the joyous, unlimited, expansive, abundant being you were born to be. To put this in the proper perspective, consider that space travel wasn't even the stuff of far-out science fiction back when we still believed the world was flat; just imagine what will fall within the realm of "possible" once we are no longer under the hypnosis of the superstition of materialism.

Here are a few of the most common core perceptions and beliefs that make up the old-world view of life, the universe, and the experience of being human:

- Action alone is the primary means for achieving any desired result, or accomplishing any goal.

- The financial reward I deserve is proportionate with the level of effort and hard work I am willing to apply.

- There is only a limited pie and we all have to fight for our share.

- I am a three-dimensional being, living in a three-dimensional world. Things that are born into this realm of space and time are the only things that exist.

- "Reality" is an objective phenomenon that all human beings perceive in the same way.

- My senses reflect accurately the nature of reality; only those things that I can see, hear, touch, smell, or taste are *real*.

- I am limited in the amount of success I can create by circumstances such as my level of education or current financial resources.

- We live in a finite universe, where there are only a finite number of resources to be divided among an ever-growing population. There are only so many high-paying careers, only so many companies that get funded, and only so many jobs and so much money to go around.

- In this world, there are haves and have-nots. Those who are already prosperous are, by definition, depriving me of my portion of prosperity.

- My emotional reactions—and, therefore, the degree to which I experience fulfillment or frustration, personal power or powerlessness—are inextricably tied to the conditions in which I find myself. In other words, I have no choice but to react to the world around me.

I want to suggest that these outdated perceptions of life are every bit as rampant, and as limiting, as the fifteenth-century superstition that the world was flat. Because in the same way that we now know not only that the world is round, but that it is a highly intelligent, spherical planet orbiting the sun in one of countless solar systems throughout an infinite universe, there is an equal quantum leap in understanding the nature of the universe and our place in it that is waiting to be embraced. As human beings, we are both physical and metaphysical. As noted by physicist Niels Bohr, who received the Nobel Prize in Physics for his foundational contributions to quantum theory, in Professor Karen Barad's 2007 work entitled *Meeting the Universe Halfway*,[4] "Everything we call real is made of things that cannot be regarded as real. If quantum mechanics hasn't profoundly shocked you, you haven't understood it yet." In the same way our hand has a front side and a back side, our human experience takes place in both the outer world of form and phenomenon, and in the inner world of energy.

Turn your attention inward, and you may begin to notice that you can actually feel the energy that is pulsating throughout your body; that is moving along with your breath; that is beaming out from behind your eyes. Your body and your breath—as well as your thoughts, feelings, ideas, beliefs, and desires—are all nothing but energy. It may be invisible to the eye, but it is received by everyone and everything around you, because all energy vibrates at a particular frequency, and this vibration can be felt, even if it can't be seen. Every sentient being, including people, animals, and plants—even molecules of water—is responsive to energy. Throughout the 1990s, Dr. Masaru Emoto, a Japanese doctor of alternative medicine, performed a series of experiments that confirmed this responsiveness dramatically.

In these experiments, petri dishes containing small samples of water were deliberately exposed to different frequencies of energy generated by a wide variety of thoughts, words, music, and even prayers. Some of the stimuli were, by nature, soothing and healing, while others were violent or even hateful. Immediately following this exposure, Emoto and his team quickly froze the water samples and examined the ice crystals that formed in each one. Their remarkable discoveries are now documented in pictures in Emoto's landmark book *The Hidden Messages in Water.*[5]

In short, the water samples that had been exposed to harmonious and loving thoughts and intentions, such as "I love you" or "You're beautiful," froze into crystals that looked like well-organized and symmetrical snowflakes, while those that were exposed to violent or hateful thoughts, such as "I hate you" or "You're ugly," did not form snowflakes but froze instead as jagged, chaotic sprays of water. Emoto's experiment accomplished what he had set out to do, proving that every thought, word, and intention we offer communicates a particular energy frequency that—while invisible to the eye—is powerful enough to change the very molecular structure of water, including the water that makes up more than 70 percent of our own bodies. From the time of our earliest socialization, most of us were taught to value the visible world of substance and form, but we are now coming to realize that even the most tangible aspects of our material world are sourced in energy.

If you take a moment to view the surroundings you find yourself in right now, your eyes will most likely fixate on the things that are tangible, like the walls, the floor, the desk, the lamp on the desk. . . . What is less obvious, at least initially, is that everything that appears material is actually surrounded by empty space. And what goes completely unnoticed by the naked eye is easily seen through a high-powered microscope, which reveals that even what appears to be solid and static isn't material at all, but made up of a sea of energy that is constantly moving and ever-changing.

> Even what appears to be solid and static isn't material at all,
> but made up of a sea of energy that is constantly moving and
> ever-changing.

Exploring the Hidden Realm of Energy

For hundreds of years, physicists and scientists have been documenting how energy, not matter, is the basis of everything that exists in our universe. In the mid-twentieth century, for example, Nobel Prize–winning physicist Werner Heisenberg forever upended the myth of Isaac Newton's "clockwork universe," in which all events were viewed as being as predictable and predetermined as the ticking of a clock. In what would become a fundamental pillar in our new quantum understanding of the world, Heisenberg discovered that nothing in the world of form has either a definite position or a predictable trajectory, and that in the very act of watching it, the observer affects the reality he is observing.[6] In physics, this phenomenon is known as the "observer effect."

Even things that appear to our senses as solid, impenetrable, and material—such as rocks, trees, and the chair you are sitting in—are made up entirely of energy. For centuries, physicists have known about dark matter, the elusive "substance" that cannot be directly observed because it emits no light or energy; but in his 2011 prize-winning book *The 4 Percent Universe*, scientific writer and Guggenheim Fellowship recipient Richard Panek quantifies what could not previously be measured. "Over the past few decades," he explains, "a handful of scientists have been racing to explain a disturbing aspect of our universe: only 4 percent of it consists of the matter that makes up you, me, our books, and every star and planet. The rest is completely unknown."[7] Modern science now has a framework for understanding what mystics have long believed: only a fraction of the consciousness that is us—4 percent, according to Panek—manifests as the physical forms we have come to think of ourselves as being. And a full 96 percent of the consciousness that we truly are exists as pure, unmanifested, energetic potential—formless, malleable, and unbounded.

Yes, you are a physical being made up of flesh, blood, bone, cells, and molecules, but the physical aspect of you represents only the tip of the proverbial iceberg of the expansive being that you truly are. You are pure, unbounded consciousness that is temporarily focused, here and now, in your body, with your unique catalog of life experiences, dreams, and desires, and for the span of this particular lifetime.

You are pure, unbounded consciousness that is temporarily focused, here and now, in your body, with your unique catalog of life experiences, dreams, and desires, and for the span of this particular lifetime.

Okay, let me guess. Having read that, there is probably some part of you that's thinking, "Well, Christy, I certainly don't *feel* unbounded. . . . I have a mortgage to pay, a job I have to report to, kids to put through college, and maybe even a college degree that I myself worked hard to earn that is not exactly the golden ticket I was told it would be." If any of the above has been or currently is your experience, don't worry. You are certainly not alone in any of those perceptions, and the good news is, you are not locked into them either. Let's continue to break down some of the components that cause us—all-powerful, eternal, and infinitely creative human beings—to relate to ourselves as mere shadows of who we really are.

You Are Much More Than You Know

Think about the aspects of yourself that you define as your "personality"—the unique attributes you possess, the knowledge you've gained as a result of the experiences you've lived, and the labels and roles you identify with and have attached your sense of self to. Now, consider that all of this represents only 4 percent of the broader consciousness that you truly are. What this means is that whatever answer immediately springs to mind when I ask "Who are you?"—whether your reply is "I am a parent." "I am a student," "I am a business owner," or "I am unemployed"—does not even *begin* to define you. These are roles you play, costumes you wear, and modes of self-expression that you participate in; certainly each of them provides an avenue for you to both give and receive attention, energy, and love. But when we view ourselves, others, and the world only from the limited perspective of the personality, we mistakenly believe that only what our senses can perceive is real, and we think that's all there is. And in so doing, we completely miss the big picture.

To define ourselves only by the content of our résumés or the sum of our life experiences is to relinquish all of our power and control to the conditions that surround us: we simply respond positively to positive conditions and negatively to negative conditions—all the while remaining oblivious to the fact that we are co-creators of the conditions that assemble around us, and as such, we always have the power to change them. When we see ourselves as separate individuals rather than as vitally important parts of an interconnected whole, we assign all our creative power to a source outside of ourselves. Our destiny feels out of our control, and in the hands of some force that we perceive as more powerful than ourselves, whether we call it God, fate, karma, or luck. And as a result, our experience of life is that it's something that happens *to* us; something that we must react to, be on guard against, or "make the best of."

When we only give credence to the aspects of ourselves that can be observed and measured by our human senses—and when we discount the broader, nonphysical origins of who we are as energy and consciousness—we feel unfairly judged against other people whom we perceive as having more resources, talent, or advantages than we do. We become slaves to our own self-judgments and comparisons, and either fight to prove that we are better than our peers, or decide that we aren't and suffer greatly in our self-condemnation. This is the level of consciousness where human beings—feeling so utterly powerless—take turns playing the role of victim and martyr, and where low-level emotions such as jealousy, envy, greed, and vindictiveness abound. Philosopher and author Eckhart Tolle describes this state of being as one in which the "pain-body" runs the show, and in which our choices are unconsciously dictated by a reactivation of old emotional pain. Tolle explains, "The pain-body consists of trapped life energy that has split off from your total energy field and has temporarily become autonomous through the unnatural process of mind identification."[8]

When this is the low level of consciousness we choose to make our "reality," we easily fall prey to addiction—such as eating too much, drinking too much, using recreational drugs, shopping, gambling, or even overambition or workaholism—as we strive to attain the external rewards that we've been taught will fulfill us. Look around, and you'll see just how many of your fellow humans are caught up in the chase for the bigger house, the next rung on the corporate ladder, the perfect life partner, or the next lavish vacation—only to discover when they get there that those things in and of themselves have no power to make us happy.

Now, if all of this is sounding pretty bleak, take heart, because an entirely different experience of life is waiting for you—and it's one that can unfold in an instant, since it requires only a shift in consciousness. As you open up to the possibility that you are much more than just a personality crammed into a flesh suit—and as you daringly begin to consider that you are in actuality a universal being, a son or daughter of the life force from whence everything has come and to which everything will return—a whole new world opens up for you, literally and figuratively.

> You are much more than just a personality crammed into a flesh suit. You are a universal being, a son or daughter of the life force from whence everything has come and to which everything will return.

The Law of Pure Potentiality

Your success in integrating the information provided throughout this book will hinge upon your willingness to consider that there exists no single, objective definition of "reality," and that each of us, in fact, creates our own unique experience of reality as a result of the particular lenses through which we perceive life. You are an integral, inextricable part of a much larger whole—by whatever name you call it: God, the universe, Mother Nature, life force energy, your inner being, or Fred. You are pure potentiality, manifested in physical form. Observe what arises within you as I suggest that you were something long before you donned the personality you now know yourself to be; that you are much more than the name by which you introduce yourself; and that the essence of you will remain long after your personality and body are no longer providing temporary housing for your life force.

As you open yourself up to this expanded level of consciousness, you become aware that the entire universe, yourself included, is made up of energy, and that you are engaged in a constant dance with the energies that are moving through you, from you, and around you. You begin to see that in this universe where there is an abundance of energy, the concept of lack is something that is entirely man-made. There is no limitation to the sun's power, to the amount of fresh air that is generated by our earth's plants, or to the potential of those plants to regenerate. Evidence of our abundance is all around us; but when we are disconnected from this truth, when we buy into and believe the lie of scarcity and limitation, then sure enough, scarcity and limitation become our reality. Yes, your perception is *that* powerful.

You, at all levels of your being—physically, emotionally, mentally—are engaged with the entire universe in a symphony of energy that is always changing. And the quality of your life experience—your health and vitality, your financial abundance, the level of joy or unhappiness you feel in each day—is always a reflection of the quality of energy you are *allowing* to flow through and from you in every moment. And more importantly, you have the power to consciously direct your energy by choosing the thoughts, emotions, attitudes, and reactions you most consistently offer—and in so doing, can cause a powerful shift in the quality of the energy, experiences, and conditions that you draw into your life.

This is a participatory universe, and the way you choose to participate in it determines the reality that unfolds in your experience. Most people's perception of life is that things happen in the outer world that cause us to offer an internal reaction in response, but I assert that the opposite is true: Every creation begins in the invisible realm of consciousness—and then, through a series of definable and very predictable steps, eventually manifests itself in the concrete world of form.

Now, I know this perspective might raise some objections—particularly in extreme cases, such as innocent children who are killed in wars, or those who are victimized by one of the many other atrocities that are erupting around the globe—but regardless of the circumstances we were born into, we always have the power to create a different reality. I was recently at an event hosted by the Unstoppable Foundation—a cause that I am passionate about and to which my husband and I make a charitable contribution each year—and heard the story of one young woman who illustrates this point profoundly.

Raised in a poor village in Kenya in East Africa, where all women are destined to be circumcised, this woman was determined in her belief that she deserved a better life, and ran away from home. Driven by her desire to experience more happiness, joy, and fulfillment than her previous circumstances would allow, this woman transcended "the way it was," and brought her highest vision into reality. Having earned her high school diploma and now attending college, she is actively giving back to the community she was born into through her affiliation with the Unstoppable Foundation, which is committed to giving girls the opportunity to get an education so they can better their lives. This young woman held steady to a dream that she believed was possible even in the face of stark evidence to the contrary, and, as a result, completely re-created her experience of reality. In this same way, every observation, perception, and conclusion you entertain in the privacy of your own heart and mind eventually manifests as an experience that you call "reality." And the reality that manifests reflects the energy frequency that is most dominant within you at every phase of this unfolding.

To understand exactly how this is so, let's explore the three main factors that are at work behind every act of creation—and to make it really tangible, let's explore it in the context of a common everyday scenario:

Thoughts + Feelings + Action = Manifestation

For the sake of understanding this formula in real-life terms, imagine that you've just been asked to give an important presentation on behalf of your company at an upcoming conference that is several months away. What you may not realize is that long before you ever step foot onto that stage or utter the first word, the thoughts, feelings, attitudes, moods, and actions that you offer in relation to this subject will set into motion a particular frequency of energies that will play out when the time comes to participate in the actual event. In other words, how your presentation will ultimately unfold when you give it in real time has *everything* to do with the energy you offered about it at every stage of its unfolding—and the quality of thoughts that you most frequently generate when considering this upcoming event is the first essential component in this formula to consider.

As the clergywoman who prayed with my friend Mary Morrissey all those years ago clearly understood, everything, and I mean *everything*, that has ever been manifested in the visible world of form—whether it's something wanted, like a thriving business venture, or something unwanted, such as the loss of that business—was first conceived in the invisible realm of thought. The late, great Stephen Covey brilliantly articulated this truth in his now-iconic *The 7 Habits of Highly Effective People:* "All things are created twice," he notes. "First in the mind, and then in reality." Consider for just a moment the staggering number of thoughts you *could* offer in response to your company's request of you to give that important presentation, and you'll see that you have the power to choose thoughts that would cause you to feel horrified or glorified. And the vast difference in the quality of your experience has only to do with the quality or frequency of energy that the thought you choose evokes within you.

When the thoughts you offer are in alignment with something you want or something you already believe in, their energy is high, light, fast-moving, and they feel fabulous when you think them. And on the other side of this spectrum, thoughts like *Why me? This is too much work*, or *I'll never succeed*, feel horrible or even paralyzing, because they are laden with resistance. Thoughts like these are steeped in lack-consciousness, and the perception that we are in any way lacking never feels good. The energy of your desired outcome is moving fast in one direction—in this case, maybe it's a desire to feel content at work, or to deliver a knockout presentation. If you offer up thoughts that doubt, undermine, or oppose the outcome you want to create, an internal tug-of-war ensues.

Earlier this year, a longtime career goal was realized for me when I was asked to give a presentation on the TEDx stage. Knowing that only those who are considered to have "ideas worth sharing" are invited to give a TED talk, I was honored and initially really excited. Then one day, after I'd submitted all the paperwork and had penned an outline for the eight-minute talk I wanted to give, I sat down to memorize what I'd written and caught myself red-handed in the middle of a thought that was in absolute opposition to the outcome I wanted to create:

I can't do this, I heard the voice in my head say. *I'm an inspirational speaker, not a memorization speaker.* My husband happened to walk into the room at that very moment and asked me how it was going. I told him, "This is really hard." The instant the words left my lips, and before he could utter a word in response, I quickly countered, "No! This is easy." In that moment I made a decision about how my experience was going to be. I decided it would be easy and that I would give an amazing, inspirational speech, even though preparing for it would require an entirely different method than I was used to. From that moment on, the memorization was easy for me, because of the thoughts I offered about it. And when the time came to take the stage, I was thrilled with how seamlessly I delivered my talk.

> There are no neutral thoughts, because with each thought we offer, we are adding to the energy that will culminate in the ultimate manifestation we are working toward.

There are no neutral thoughts, because with each thought we offer, we are adding to the energy that will culminate in the ultimate manifestation we are working toward. The following proverb—which is so universal that it's been attributed to luminaries as diverse as Lao Tzu, Ralph Waldo Emerson, and Margaret Thatcher—sums up the power of thought quite eloquently:

> *"Watch your thoughts; they become words.*
> *Watch your words; they become actions.*
> *Watch your actions; they become habits.*
> *Watch your habits; they become character.*
> *Watch your character; it becomes your destiny."*

The one missing ingredient in this beautiful description of how consciousness manifests into concrete form and thoughts become things is actually the next stage in the unfolding of every manifestation: feeling.

What Grows in the Garden of Your Mind

Going back to our example about being asked to deliver a presentation at an upcoming conference, it's fairly easy to make the connection between our knee-jerk or habitual patterns of thought and our chances of succeeding or failing in any endeavor. But in order to understand just how powerfully the quality of our thoughts impacts the quality of the results we ultimately achieve, we have to fill in the essential link missing from the adage I quoted above: the reason thoughts are so influential is not because of their content (and, by the way, their ability to influence has nothing whatsoever to do with whether or not the thought is actually true). Thoughts are powerful because they generate within us correspondent *feelings*, oftentimes in such rapid-fire succession that we can't tell which came first.

If you've ever caught yourself rehashing a situation or replaying in your mind an encounter that hurt, disappointed, or annoyed you, it's likely that you've already noticed two very important things about the power of your thoughts. First, the more airtime you give to them, the more vivid and detailed they become; and second, the mind cannot tell the difference between a thought about something "real," and a thought about something you are remembering from the past or imagining in the future. When your heart races and your palms sweat while watching that scary movie, the fear you feel is no less real than if the events you're seeing on screen were actually happening to you.

The thoughts we think, whether "real" or imagined, flood our minds with images that have the power to trigger the entire range of both good-feeling and lousy-feeling human emotions. Our thoughts are like seeds, and our minds are like a fertile field of soil that will nourish any seed that we plant within it—whether it's a seed from a beautiful rose-bush or the seed of a pernicious weed. The soil will nourish it regardless, and in time, that tiny seed will grow into a mature plant that is fertile enough to produce its own seeds.

> **Our thoughts are like seeds, and our minds are like a fertile field of soil that will nourish any seed that we plant within it—whether it's a seed from a beautiful rosebush or the seed of a pernicious weed.**

In this way, our thoughts give rise to a field of emotions that are nourished and strengthened by our continued attention to them, creating a self-generating feedback loop: particular thoughts generate predictable feelings, which then inspire more thoughts that intensify and reinforce those feelings. Said another way, the thoughts we think most frequently lead to chronic moods that can become so differentiated that we actually label them with a diagnosis. But this final manifestation—whether it's an abundant, fragrant rosebush or a malevolent weed—

began as something so small that it was barely perceptible. The thoughts you most dominantly offer engender your most dominant emotional states, and the more attention you give to these, the stronger and more resilient they grow. For better, and for worse.

What distinguishes a pleasurable emotion like love from a painful emotion like sadness or rage is the frequency and speed at which its energy vibrates. The vibrations we offer in every moment are transmitted through the airwaves like radio signals, and are registered by everyone and everything around us. In the same way that a magnet is attractive to steel, we draw energy into our lives that resonates at a similar frequency to our own. As human beings, we are like walking, breathing energy towers that are in every moment broadcasting a frequency to everyone and everything we are in relationship with—and that includes our careers. The quality of the energy we send out determines the quality of the people, situations, circumstances, events, and experiences that we draw into our lives in response.

So, going back to our imaginary presentation, it's fairly easy to see how upbeat, inspired, positive thoughts lead to high-flying emotions that can set a positive flow of energy into motion—but what impact could this possibly have on the quality of the presentation we actually deliver? Enter the third stage in the equation that guides every process of becoming: action.

The Tipping Point

Back in high school chemistry class, you probably learned that certain chemicals, when mixed together, generate so much heat and internal pressure that in time they will inevitably explode. Well, the combination of particular thoughts with the corresponding feelings they trigger—which then trigger more vivid thoughts and intense feelings—gives rise to its own kind of explosion: eventually, the energy created by this thought-feeling circuit builds up so much momentum that it can no longer be contained in the invisible realm of thought and emotion. Once it reaches this volatile tipping point, the energy of our dominant thoughts and emotions will seek manifestation in the physical, tangible world. In other words, it will compel us to *act*.

To understand this stage of the process of manifestation, let's revisit one last time the simple example of your company asking you to be a presenter at an upcoming conference. And for the sake of this example, let's assume also that you have taken to heart the information that I've shared with you here, and embraced the idea that thoughts really do become things—first by evoking within you certain feelings, which continue to increase in momentum until the pressure is so great that finally you cannot help but take action. And let's suppose that you have decided to apply your new understanding of this formula of manifestation to use your upcoming presentation to create the best possible outcome for yourself and for your company.

Your first order of business, of course, is to decide what the best possible outcome looks like, and to get as clear as you are able—as we explored in the previous chapter—about the portion of this ever-unfolding vision that you are able to see from your current vantage point. With this vision in your mind, and armed with the knowledge that the thoughts you offer will lead you either toward or away from it, you deliberately scan your environment, your memory, your imagination, and anything else you can think of for thoughts whose energy resonates with the outcome you want to create. Maybe you ask yourself questions similar to those that were posed in the previous chapter—questions like "What would my ideal outcome look like, and how would it feel to have already attained it?" or "What unique strengths and insights have equipped me perfectly to succeed in this event?" As you ask these questions and become open to receiving answers, your vision will expand, like roots germinating from a seed, until soon its first sprouts break ground, seeking the sunlight above.

And sunlight is to your budding seedling, you now understand, what good-feeling emotions are to your brand-new vision: a source of nourishment that is absolutely essential if your plant is to survive. Knowing this, you consciously and deliberately encourage feelings that inspire interest, that light you up, that alert you to new possibilities, while steering clear of feelings that undermine or contradict your desire.

You indulge in thoughts for the singular reason that those thoughts feel good. And amazingly, the more you reach for good-feeling feelings, the more of them you find. If you allow this creative process to continue to unfold, soon more good-feeling ideas are born from those feelings. By aligning yourself energetically with the internal feeling state you want to experience as a result of your external creation, you call into being the 96 percent of you that exists as pure potential energy and allow it to infuse every action you take. You are officially on a roll.

Eventually the energy of your high-flying thoughts combined with their corresponding high-flying emotions becomes so intense that, like chemicals mixed in a bottle, the energy seeks expression in whatever way it can find, and you are compelled into action. Not action intended to please someone else or action taken simply for the sake of getting things done, but action that is inspired from the highest spiritual essence of you. This quality of action yields a dramatically different quality of results than the opposite scenario.

When we view ourselves as clumps of matter, rather than as unlimited streams of pure energy and consciousness, we tend to view action as the primary means for accomplishing goals. First we must take the action, we think, and then we'll receive the benefit of that action. But when you understand the more subtle realms of life, you come to see that the reverse is not only true, but far more effective. You can actually align in thought, emotion, and energy with your desired outcome, and that energy will draw you to the actions that will support its unfolding. Actions that are taken from a state of energetic, mental, and emotional alignment with the end goal are infinitely more powerful than those taken without this connection. In psychological terms, this state of energetic alignment or misalignment accounts for the difference between intrinsic versus external motivation.

> **You can actually align in thought, emotion, and energy with the desired outcome, and that energy will draw you to the actions that will support its unfolding.**

When we're intrinsically motivated, we are inspired toward a certain action because we are genuinely interested in, engaged with, or curious about where the action might lead. If you've ever felt so compelled to do something that *not* doing it was simply not an option, then you know the power of intrinsic motivation. You move into action for its own sake, either because of the enjoyment you anticipate the action will provide, or because the impulse to act was too strong to ignore. As its name implies, intrinsic motivation is motivation that occurs from the inside out.

Extrinsic motivation, on the other hand, is always driven by an anticipation of attaining a desired reward, or the avoidance of an unwanted consequence. Staying at a job you can't stand because you need the paycheck, or giving great customer service for the sole purpose of garnering a rave review are both examples of extrinsic motivation. When we are extrinsically motivated, there is a huge disparity between our outward behaviors and our true desires, and this split in our energy not only makes us less effective in terms of getting things done, but also drains our credibility because others can perceive when our actions are not inspired from within.

In your own life, can you tell the difference between an action taken from obligation and one that is genuinely inspired? Can you feel the difference in work that's been done begrudgingly and work that has been offered with joy in the giving? The same facial muscles are activated in both cases, but can you tell a sincere smile from a fake one? If you answered yes to even one of these questions, you must acknowledge the existence of a world beyond what can be perceived through your five senses. Although it can't be quantified or counted, this realm exerts a far greater effect on us than anything we can see or taste or touch.

No scientist can objectively measure the appreciation that comes from eating food that was prepared with love (not at the time of this writing, anyway), but most would agree that this is the stuff that makes life worth living. Fulfillment does not occur from just filling our bodies with requisite amounts of fiber and protein, and it doesn't come about from clocking in to a job each day only for the sake of making ends meet. It occurs in the experiences we have along the way, in the subtler realms of reality where inspiration arises. This is the realm where ideas are born, and are nourished in the infant stages of their becoming.

Let's recap this process of manifestation: Your consciousness gave birth to a single idea, which your mind, like a beautiful kaleidoscope, reflected into thousands of unique resonant thoughts. Those thoughts generated energy that traveled all throughout your body and mind, changing your body chemistry, your posture, and the depth of your breathing, and triggered feelings that acted like fuel to this hot, bright, internally blazing fire.

The next part of this magical unfolding is governed by a process of magnetism that we will explore in great detail throughout this book, but suffice it to say that once you have taken the steps to offer your internal feeling state on purpose, experiences that resonate with the internal environment you have created make their way to you like moths to a flame.

Creating quantum success in your career is not a result of meticulous planning or painstaking, excruciating effort. It is the result of preparing your consciousness—which is to say the thoughts, beliefs, conclusions, perceptions, and feelings that you experience in the privacy of your own heart and mind—for the success that you desire. You create it first in energy, and then all manner of people, circumstances, and resources are magnetized to the energy you offer. Most of us have been taught that achieving success comes about when we become effective at manipulating conditions into place. But this is a false conclusion. That which you define as success is a reality that is drawn into being through the power of the dominant vibration that you offer. Learning how to offer your vibration on purpose is the basis of conscious creation, and the secret to manifesting quantum success—in your career and in any other area of your life.

Everything we experience in the external, manifested world is a direct reflection of what we are experiencing within the internal world of our perception. Life is a dance between inner and outer; between the spiritual and the material; between energy and matter. This is because as human beings, we exist in multiple dimensions simultaneously. There is the part of us that is tangible and manifested—the 4 percent that exists in physical form; that interacts with other forms; that takes physical, concrete action. But underlying this physical aspect of us is our non-physical essence—the inner realm where our thoughts, beliefs, perceptions, desires, and emotions are formed. This larger, wiser part of us is always present, whether we are at rest or in motion and whether we are awake or asleep. Consciousness breathes life into the concrete, and our physical surroundings are a visible out-picturing, a manifestation, of our moment-to-moment internal reality. Our inner and outer worlds are inseparable, in the same way that the front of your hand is inseparable from the back of your hand.

> Our inner and outer worlds are inseparable, in the same way that the front of your hand is inseparable from the back of your hand.

It is high time that we stop limiting the potential of our human experience by viewing it as a fixed and limited three-dimensional reality. However you define success—whether as an abundance of money or creativity or freedom or joy—in order to create it, you must simply embrace a broader understanding of what is really going on here, behind the illusion of what seems a purely material existence, and beyond the veil of form. When you enter the higher phases of consciousness, you know that if you want something to shift in your life, you must make the shift inside of yourself, and that the only one who can do that is you. The only thing we ever have control over is our own choosing and accepting of the vibrations with which we participate. This understanding is the key to creating not just a fabulous career, but every other experience you desire in this life.

Once you understand the world of energy and become practiced at consistently offering your energy intentionally, you will inevitably experience a shift in consciousness from lack to abundance. This is where you begin to see that you have the ability to do something other than react to the conditions in which you find yourself—or, worse, try to change those conditions so they'll evoke from you a different reaction. You discover that you have the ability to choose what you want to experience, generate that experience for yourself from within, and—through the power of your own focus—attract to yourself those people, circumstances, and events that are an energetic match to what you desire.

As you give up the outworn mind-sets of separation, lack, scarcity, and competition and make way for a broader reality to emerge, your pain-body begins to loosen its grip and you become more and more aware of the presence of the subtler dimensions from which everything arises. You have a growing awareness of the 96 percent of you that is unmanifested—that, in the words of the Bhagavad Gita, "fire cannot burn, water cannot wet, and weapons cannot cleave," the part of you that is "ancient and unborn—and therefore never dies."

Now, in case I lost you with that last reference, please know that I have no particular religious affiliation, yet find references to quantum success sprinkled within many of the world's religions. My life's work is not based on theory or religious doctrine, but on proven success principles that I've studied, applied, and taught others for almost twenty years, which are undeniably nodded to within the pages of sacred texts. These references include an understanding of what I have just described as the 96 percent of each of us that is nonphysically focused, or what some might call the spiritual aspect of life. We live in a time when science no longer denies the existence of energetic dimensions. I've also found in working with hundreds of thousands of people from all walks of life that most do have some relationship with—or at least some inkling of—this higher part of themselves. In whatever way you conceive of the aspect of you that is deeper, broader, wiser, or more enduring than your personality's limited perspective of life—this is the part of you that I will be guiding you to access throughout this book. Once this opening between your personality and your higher self occurs (or, more accurately, once the veils of perception that have blocked this opening are removed), you will begin to glimpse the tremendous power of shifting your inner world. This knowledge will return you to the driver's seat of your own life, as you reclaim the powerful creator you are and were born to be.

Understanding the World of Energy: Putting It into Action

To begin, understand that there is not one "right" way to experience the flow of spiritual energy that nourishes and sources everything in the manifested world. No special equipment is necessary, nor do you need to place yourself in any uniquely serene environment. Energy is at the basis of everything, and both harmonic and discordant energies can be experienced in every moment and in every situation—once you train yourself to tune to it, that is.

We live in a world where action is praised, to the point that many of us find ourselves frantically rushing around and multitasking, thinking that if we can get the external circumstances of our lives to look a particular way, we will finally have the success, or the fulfillment, or the joy that we're seeking. But we have this backward.

In the same way that you can't hear a whisper at a rock concert, you cannot connect with the subtle realm of energy when all your attention is focused on the world of form. To experience the hidden world of energy, you have to find a way to unwind, go within, and allow yourself to rest in a soft and easy state of simply being.

While many of you will already have a daily practice, this state of being for manifesting is best nourished through consistent meditation, mindfulness, or resting in silence. If closed-eye meditation doesn't appeal to you, you can focus your attention on the flame of a candle, or put on some peaceful music and quietly listen. Or you can follow the process outlined below, which will guide you to connect with the subtle realm of energy. (If you prefer to listen to this meditation rather than read it and follow along, please visit hyperlink www.christywhitman .com/qsbook to download free recordings of this and each of the processes described throughout this book.)

CONNECTING WITH THE HIDDEN WORLD OF ENERGY

Begin by sitting quietly in a comfortable environment where you are unlikely to be disturbed for the next fifteen or twenty minutes. Bring forth the intention to make contact with the subtle realm of consciousness, the 96 percent of you that is formless and unmanifested. Know that this broader aspect of you is a wellspring of wisdom, and the source of all your creativity, inspiration, and prosperity. With a deep breath, open yourself up to receiving all of the gifts that this broader aspect of you is always making available.

As you let go of any thoughts or expectations, allow yourself to consider that you are that infinite intelligence, that unconditional love and all-knowing wisdom, and that the creative force from which all things are born is looking out through your eyes. Sense this expanded "I" within you, this pure witnessing awareness that is always present.

Let your mind come completely to rest, to a state of inner stillness. There is nothing for you to do or to think about, and there is no result that you need to focus on achieving. Give yourself permission to simply melt into a fluid state of being. Withdraw any thoughts or concerns you may have about the outer world and allow your attention to go deep within, to merge with the larger consciousness of which we are all an integral part.

Acknowledge that this internal, witnessing aspect of you has been present with you through all of your life experiences, and trust that it has the power to fulfill your every worldly desire; that it has the power to infuse all your intentions with as much of its wisdom, power, and love as you can allow yourself to accept.

Take the next five or ten minutes to simply enjoy this inner connection—however you perceive it and however it occurs to you— knowing that the act of going within will give you access to even greater power, love, wisdom, guidance, abundance, and spiritual vision. It is fine if you do not perceive anything that you can directly feel or identify; know that contact has been made simply through your intention to make contact, and that with this, some insight, extra energy, or inspiration has been imparted to you that will unfold at the perfect time.

As you slowly transition back to your normal, wakeful state and begin to turn your attention back to your everyday life, notice whether it has a different quality, texture, or feeling. As you begin to come more fully back into your body, notice if you feel a greater sense of aliveness, or any other quality that you associate with a stronger connection to the energy source that sustains your physicality.

When you are ready, slowly open your eyes, bringing with you any and all of the gifts you received from the nonphysical aspect of you.

Note that it is not necessary to invest a lot of time in this meditation in order to begin reaping the benefits of a clearer and more sustainable connection with the energy that sustains you. In fact, it can be just as effective to take ten- or twenty-second periods several times during each day to pause, quiet your mind, and deliberately open yourself to the energetic realms where inspiration and guidance are always accessible to you.

Remember that energy is nothing that is hard to grasp; you've been sending and receiving it for all the days of your life. Energy is simply the "nonstuff" that is the basis of all that appears material, and once you become sensitive, you can experience it even when you are deeply focused in activity. Practice taking people in on all levels of their being while talking with them, and see if you can notice the exchange of energy that is being given and received in the conversation. Notice the energy exchange that is taking place between you and every situation, idea, or object that you direct your attention toward. What type of energy are you flowing toward the idea of abundance and success? As you develop greater sensitivity, you will begin to notice whether your energy feels expansive or contracted in the environments you most commonly find yourself in—and this includes the environment that you are creating within yourself. In the chapters that follow, I'll show you how to focus on the aspects of those around you that uplift you the most, and how to create your own energetic environment around yourself that will nourish and sustain you no matter where you go or what you are engaged in.

3

CONTROLLING YOUR OWN EMOTIONAL DIAL

"What I know now is that feelings are really your GPS system for life. When you're supposed to do something or not supposed to do something, your emotional guidance system lets you know. The trick is to learn to check your ego at the door and start checking your gut instead."

—OPRAH WINFREY

WHEN I WAS GROWING UP IN THE EARLY SEVENTIES, watching TV was a very different experience than it is today. You couldn't just sit back on the couch with your remote in hand and flip idly through countless stations, watching each one for only a few seconds before moving on to the next. Nope, there was more to it than that. If the station you were on was playing a Western and you were in the mood for *Charlie's Angels*, you had to actually get up out of your seat, walk across the room to the TV set, and turn the dial by hand. TV watching back then took more deliberate intention than is required nowadays, but once the family had settled on a particular show, we usually watched the whole thing through—and enjoyed it more than if we'd had the option to keep flipping through the channels haphazardly. I offer this simple metaphor because it is actually very useful in understanding the difference between creating your life on purpose, rather than creating it randomly or by default. Let me explain.

Think for a moment about the seven billion plus people who are currently inhabitants of planet earth, who have taken manifestation in this dimension of time and space where sensory experience is possible. Consider how many people of all ages, value systems, and backgrounds are living out their lives in cities, suburbs, and villages in every corner of this big blue marble. How many different versions of "reality" do you imagine are being lived among those seven billion people?

I am going to assert that no two experiences of reality are the same— not even those of two people living in the same home. I see this all the time when observing my two young children. Maxim is happy with whatever comes his way, while Alex is always on the hunt for something more. They have very different natures and different points of focus, and even though they are living in the same house, with the same parents, doing many of the same activities, the thoughts and emotions that make up each of their life experiences are very different. And if I had the ability to expand my field of vision to encompass a larger worldview, I would see that in this single moment in time, there are people who are experiencing a reality that is horrible beyond words; others who are living a joyful, even exalted experience; and those whose experiences fall at virtually every point in between.

So how can we account for this dramatic variance in the quality of our life experiences? Certainly the conditions in which we find ourselves have something to do with our degree of happiness or misery—but the question almost no one has stepped far enough back to ask is, how is it that those conditions come into our experience in the first place? Why are some people ensconced in every possible manifestation of abundance while others are toiling and struggling and still never have enough? Here is where our TV channel-flipping analogy comes in handy.

In the same way you now have access to thousands of different programs on your smart TV, all manner of life experiences, both wanted and unwanted, are available to each one of us in every moment—because each one of us has access to the full range of human emotions. And when I say the *full* range, I mean every feeling along a huge emotional spectrum, all the way from the devastating to the sublime. Every one of these emotions, and the life experience it correlates with, is as readily accessible as a channel called up by your TV remote.

> In the same way you now have access to thousands of different programs on your smart TV, all manner of life experiences, both wanted and unwanted, are available to each one of us in every moment—because each one of us has access to the full range of human emotions.

Like the satellite signals and radio waves that flow freely through the airwaves, every emotion is an energetic frequency that we have the ability to tune in to, twenty-four hours a day and seven days a week. The question is, in relation to your career, what range of emotions is your dial set to receive? And what "programs" do you find yourself tuning in to on a regular or even daily basis? Now, these are some pretty broad questions, so let's narrow it a bit.

When you bring to mind a vision of you at the center of a successful, thriving, abundant career, what are the dominant emotions that this thought conjures within you? Are they feelings of confidence and eager anticipation? Or is the bank of thoughts you have most ready access to more in the neighborhood of doubt, pessimism, or fear? When you think about the subject of money, is the dominant feeling within you one of freedom, lightness, ease, and possibility, or one of anxiety, struggle, and dread? Understanding the emotional responses that come up most frequently when you consider your own career success is vital. Because, as we explored in the previous chapter, your experience of reality is generated based on the energetic frequency you most dominantly offer—and your emotions provide tangible, visceral feedback about whether you are in a state of alignment with or resistance to your own desire.

The Law of Attraction

Everything that manifests in the physical world does so because like energies have been drawn together. This is the essence of the Law of Attraction, which states that whatever energy we broadcast out into the universe is joined by and gathers to itself energies that are harmonic or resonant in frequency. For example, if you hit a C major chord on a piano, every other key on the piano that is tuned to the chord of C will quiver in response to the notes that have been sounded. Whether it's in the realm of sound and light, or in the realm of emotion and thought, frequencies that resonate at a similar vibration are magnetized together. This same concept holds true in the inner realm of your beliefs, desires, thoughts, and emotions: a desire that is unobstructed by a contradictory belief creates good-feeling emotions as it moves with velocity along the path toward its fulfillment.

As you're reading these words, see if you can recall a time when you felt eager, excited, or passionate about something; a time when you were in a state of positive expectation about what was to come. If you allow that feeling to gain a little momentum within you, you may notice that it brings with it a rushing, enlivening sensation. This is an example of energy that is moving at a high frequency and rate of speed because it is not being slowed down by a contradictory thought, emotion, or belief. And if you were to now recall the sensation of feeling disappointed or rejected, or of dreading something you feared was not going to turn out well, that rushing feeling would quickly be replaced by a much duller, denser sensation. This is an example of energy that is traveling at a lower, slower frequency because it is moving through resistance. Your emotions let you know how high and fast—or how low and slow—a vibration you are offering in every moment, and in relation to every important person and subject in your life: the higher and more allowing your vibration, the better you feel.

When we're in a state of allowing, all the ideas, inspiration, and opportunities that we need to manifest our goals flow to us easily, as effortlessly as the act of breathing. Emotions are simply energy in motion, and like the notes produced by a musical instrument, each one vibrates at a particular frequency.

Emotional Channel-Surfing

The idea that different emotions transmit different frequencies of vibration is hardly new. The early research conducted by psychologist George Mandler that led to the development of biofeedback, which uses instruments to measure the physical signs and symptoms associated with different emotional states—such as heart rate, body temperature, and muscle tension—dates back to the late 1950s. Nearly forty years later, physician and researcher David Hawkins published his breakthrough book *Power vs. Force,* which compiled the results of thousands of studies conducted using kinesiology as a tool for measuring the differing vibrational frequencies of emotions, perceptions, attitudes, worldviews, and spiritual beliefs, demonstrated that each of our emotional states generates a particular response in the human body and energy field. Not surprisingly, emotions such as peace, joy, and love register at the highest level of the scale, while the emotions of guilt and shame resonate at the lowest frequency.[9]

More recently, Law of Attraction teachers Esther and Jerry Hicks developed what they termed an "Emotional Guidance Scale," which they published in their 2004 work *Ask and It Is Given*.[10] As you read through this most recent version of the list, notice that the vibration generated by each subsequent emotional state feels a bit like turning your dial to receive progressively lower, slower, and denser channels:

1. Joy/Knowledge/Empowerment/Freedom/Love/Appreciation
2. Passion
3. Enthusiasm/Eagerness/Happiness
4. Positive Expectation/Belief
5. Optimism
6. Hopefulness
7. Contentment
8. Boredom
9. Pessimism
10. Frustration/Impatience/Irritation
11. Overwhelm
12. Disappointment
13. Doubt
14. Worry
15. Blame
16. Discouragement
17. Anger
18. Revenge
19. Hatred/Rage
20. Jealousy
21. Insecurity/Guilt/Unworthiness
22. Fear/Grief/Depression/Despair/Powerlessness

Can you see how each of these emotional states offers up an entirely different experience of life—in the same way that every TV channel broadcasts its own range of programming? Every emotion we can possibly experience resides on a particular channel, and the channel we tune to makes us receptive to a particular range of experiences, emotions, opportunities, situations, circumstances, and conditions. If you choose the Abundance and Prosperity channel as it relates to your career, and you stay focused and attuned to that channel without letting anything or anyone pull you from that frequency, you will feel more abundant and prosperous in your career. But how many people do you know who keep their attention purely focused on the channel of what they *do* want to create, rather than focused on what they don't?

> How many people do you know who keep their attention purely
> focused on the channel of what they do want to create, rather
> than focused on what they don't?

The entire range of emotional channels is accessible to all of us in each moment, but in relation to the area of their career expression, many people keep themselves stuck watching a very limited selection of programs, toggling among the Overwhelm, Resentment, and Martyr channels, with only an occasional pit stop at Happy. But this need not be the case, because in the same way that you adjust your TV remote to a certain channel to find your favorite program, you can determine the quality of your experience in each key aspect of your life by paying attention to the emotions you are generating at any moment—and making the decision to choose that channel on purpose.

Now, if all of this sounds a little "out there," please stay with me and you'll see that it's really not. In fact, I'm certain that you have had many personal experiences with the exact phenomenon that I am describing here. For example, call to mind someone who is important to you—maybe it's a family member or a spouse or a good friend—and deliberately conjure feelings of appreciation and love for that person. Stay with those feelings for a minute or so; then take a deep breath, and this time deliberately bring to mind when you experienced being angry with this person, or felt worried about them in some way.

From this simple exercise, it's pretty easy to see how your experience of a person changes as a result of the emotional state you are in when you think about them, just as an object looks different when viewed through different-colored lenses. If you're in a state of appreciation when you think about something or someone, you'll actually have access to different memories, ideas, and images than if you're in a state of doubt or insecurity. The same holds true when you think about your career, about the money you desire to make, about the project you're currently working on, or about your own qualifications. Your experience of reality changes as your perceptions change, and this is where things become very exciting.

Because we are each born with the incredible gift of free will, we have the unique opportunity to think—and therefore to feel—on purpose. We can adjust our own emotional dial, and in so doing call forth an entirely new experience of life. On every subject and in every interaction, you have the option of focusing on the aspects that evoke good-feeling emotions or the aspects that evoke bad-feeling emotions. And the choice you make most often will determine the quality of your experience in that part of your life.

This sounds easy enough, right? Simply focus on the attributes of yourself and others that make you feel the best, and you will attract more of that energy into your life . . . but why is this sometimes so difficult to apply? The answer to this is that, because most of us are not conscious that we have the power to deliberately direct our attention, we unwittingly allow it to be hijacked by whatever interaction or circumstance we happen to find ourselves in. All of us have developed certain ruts in our thinking that we unconsciously fall into anytime we encounter a particular person or situation. For example, consider the subject of taxes, and notice the automatic cascade of thoughts and emotions that is triggered within you. To change the stations that are preset, so to speak, on our emotional dials with regard to certain situations and subjects, we first have to locate where those emotional hot buttons are, and then make a deliberate decision to think and feel about these subjects differently than we have in the past. The following 3-step exercise will support you in strengthening your ability to change channels on purpose.

STEP #1: IDENTIFY THE CHANNEL YOU MOST OFTEN TUNE INTO

Begin by reflecting on some aspect of your career where you are not completely satisfied or would like things to be different, and honestly take a look at what emotional "channel" you spend most of your time tuned to. Are you tuned to the Struggle channel? The Frustration channel? The Overwhelmed channel? What is the emotional or energetic essence of the channel you're tuned to currently?

STEP #2: IDENTIFY A BETTER-FEELING CHANNEL

Next, realizing that there are countless other frequencies that you *could* choose to tune to, allow yourself to identify what channel you would prefer. If this area of your life were exactly the way you want it to be, what emotions do you believe would be most dominant in your experience? Would you be tuned to the Financial Freedom and Abundance channel? The Vitality channel? The Inspired Action channel?

STEP #3: TAKE BACK THE CONTROLS

Finally, just like I had to do as a kid back in the 1970s, when we actually had to get up and walk across the room to watch the show we wanted, take your hand and physically act out the motion of changing your emotional dial to the new frequency of your choice. As you do, allow yourself to feel the vibration of this new channel. How does it feel to reside here? What are you now inspired to do differently that you didn't do before? What new choices, ideas, or opportunities are available on this new wavelength? And in the coming weeks, anytime you notice your mood begin to take a dip or that your thoughts are becoming worrisome or negative, remind yourself that there are an infinite number of emotional channels that you can access simply by directing your focus there. You are *that* powerful!

Locating Your Emotional Presets

From the time we are very young, and well before we use language to talk, we are taking the emotional and energetic pulse of our households and imprinting at unconscious levels the moods, desires, and expectations of the other humans around us. And because as babies and toddlers we are dependent on our caregivers for our very survival, we often develop more sensitivity to the feelings of others than to our own.

From a very young age, we contort and control our own emotional responses in order to appease the adults on whom we depend. Add to this tendency the familiar cultural messages so many of us received, such as "Boys don't cry," "You don't need a new toy," or "Good girls don't get angry," and we discover yet another barrier to feeling and responding to the wisdom of our own emotional guidance. It's only natural to want to feel that we understand and are understood by the people closest to us, but in becoming empathic to their chronic moods and dominant opinions, we unwittingly take ourselves off our own path.

Fast-forward fifteen or twenty years from early childhood: now we have not only the expectations of our own families to contend with, but we have friends, lovers, teachers, bosses, and society as a whole all guiding us toward some image of what it means to be productive or successful. There are also the impersonal thought forms, beliefs, and opinions that flow through the airwaves of mass consciousness that subtly influence our perceptions of everything from the economy to the weather to the president. If we allow these external forces to guide the forward motion of our own lives, our self-perceptions become clouded, and our ability to solve problems and to connect to bigger possibilities is diminished. One of the reasons that it is so imperative to look within and to seek resonance with the broader, wiser part of us that exists at the core of our being is because of just how much each of us has been trained to look outside ourselves for answers to the questions that life inevitably brings to light. Black-and-white thinking, catastrophizing, and organizing our actions according to "shoulds" laid out by ourselves and others are all examples of the mental pitfalls that can arise from prioritizing outside opinions, emotions, and perspectives above our own.

The more we allow ourselves to be guided by these external influences—and, subsequently, by our own flawed patterns of thought that keep these influences alive—the more estranged from our own guidance system we become. In personal relationships and at work, we may suddenly find ourselves tuned to an emotional channel that does not resonate with who we are or where we are headed, having no idea how we got there. This is precisely how, without even realizing it, we give others power over the way we feel. And it's also how, if this goes on long enough, our emotional responses become so habituated and reflexive that we may feel we have no control over them. Like a Pavlovian dog, we simply react to a particular stimulus by offering a predictable response.

To create the career—and the life—that you desire, you must reclaim your inherent ability to feel on purpose.

To create the career—and the life—that you desire, you must reclaim your inherent ability to feel on purpose. This is done through mastering the power of your own individual focus, and by making a decision about what channel you wish to tune in to along your emotional dial. Once you get the hang of this, there is nothing that is not possible for you.

Flipping the Switch (Hint: It's on the Inside)

First, I'd like to give you something to consider: If someone compliments you, must you automatically feel flattered? And if someone insults you, do you have to become insulted? Most would say yes. Unless we've been taught that we have the power to direct our attention (and therefore our creative energy) on purpose, we often feel at the mercy of those around us.

So, for example, if you walk into a work environment that's orderly and cooperative, your automatic response might be to feel at ease and to perhaps give yourself permission to be at your most productive. But if that environment turns gossipy or mean-spirited and you haven't yet learned how to redirect your attention, your creative energy could easily become diluted or redirected. In reacting to the chaos around you, you may find yourself putting out fires or trying to keep the peace instead of tending to the realization of your own goals and desires. It takes attention to remain focused on the bigger picture of what you're committed to creating—especially in the presence of those who seem like they will stop at nothing to pull you off track.

The transitional period just before I left my corporate career to pursue my passion for coaching full-time provided valuable on-the-job training in the skill of maintaining a strong internal focus in the face of compelling external distractions. On the one hand, I had never been happier: in coaching, I had finally found a career expression that was meaningful to me and provided upliftment to others; my personal growth was skyrocketing at an incredible rate; and—to top it all off—I was newly in love with my soon-to-be husband, Frederic.

When I wasn't at my eight-to-five job, where I had achieved a lot of success and accolades as a sales training manager, I was happily engaged in studying and applying the laws of deliberate creation, coaching others to do the same, and working out the details of my unfolding vision to move to Montreal to live with Frederic and to start my own coaching practice. When I was at work, however, I was met by constant opposition to all the forward motion I was creating in my life. This opposition was steadily applied by my boss, Dan, who was known, not so affectionately, by the other managers as "Eagle," because he made it his business to watch over every little thing we did.

Eagle's office was just a few doors down from mine (in which he had been seen going through my personal things on more than one occasion, by the way), but he watched over me with an especially sharp eye anytime I was training a class. I enjoyed my role as a trainer, and loved sharing insights and tools that I knew would help the salespeople succeed. And, because prior to accepting the role of training manager I had been one of the company's most successful sales reps to date, I had a lot of experience to draw from when teaching. But even though I earned rave reviews from every training class I'd taught, Eagle wrote me up for not following the curriculum verbatim, and required me to check in with him prior to teaching each module, which struck me as a needless expenditure of time and made me feel constricted and resistant. I complied, but his attempts to derail my success didn't stop there. Instead, he'd give me assignments for creating sales models that were destined to fail, and when I presented them at staff meetings would reprimand me for having come up with *his* idea.

Basically, Eagle did all he could to make my life at work a living hell—but when his interference went beyond our shared office and into my private life, I knew he was someone I'd have to contend with. Once, after approving vacation time that I'd requested months in advance, he went onto my personal website, where he figured out that the reason I had asked for the time off was that I was scheduled for a book signing in New York—and promptly revoked the vacation time that had already been approved.

Eventually, I filed a complaint with the company's HR department— only to discover that several claims filed by other employees were open and still pending. At that moment, I realized that depending on where and how I focused my attention, I could perceive Eagle as an insurmountable adversary who would stand in the way of my goals or as a golden opportunity to sharpen my teeth as a deliberate creator.

Because I had no doubt about my skills and had received plenty of feedback that I was doing a good job at work, I decided to view Eagle not as an obstacle to fulfilling my vision of becoming a coach, but as someone who was adding fuel to my growing internal fire. Had it not been for his incessant harassment, my desire to work for myself in a field that empowered and inspired people might not have gathered the traction that I needed to successfully make the jump—or the focus that was required to continue building my business at each important stage of its development.

It would have been really easy for me to allow my boss's negativity to drain my energy and enthusiasm, so to prevent this from happening I deliberately chose to focus only on the positive aspects of my job. Daily I would make a list of all the things I was grateful for about it: I was making good money; I did not have to work on weekends; I lived close enough to where I worked that I could go home for lunch and to recharge; I had become friends with a couple of my coworkers who were fun to play with. . . . Anytime I found myself tempted to tune in to the default channel of the company—that of being a bitter, disgruntled employee—I would read this list, knowing that if I allowed myself to get off track emotionally during my workday, it would affect everything else I was committed to creating and experiencing in my life. I made a conscious decision to no longer give my boss or anyone else the power to choose my emotions, and proclaimed myself the only one with the ability to choose my emotional channel.

I share this story for a couple of reasons. First, I've seen many people be completely caught off guard when, after clarifying a new career vision and taking steps toward it, they encountered resistance from those around them. This resistance may come in the form of teasing, passive-aggressive jabs, or—as in the case of Eagle—overt hostility, criticism, and interference. This type of backlash is more common than you might think. Coworkers, friends, and even your own spouse are accustomed to relating to you at a certain level, and when you decide to play a bigger game, your resolve can be threatening; they may consciously or unconsciously say or do things to bring you back down to their level. But because you have the power to choose your own point of focus, you can take this opposition as a sign to retreat, or you can use it as a catalyst to pull you forward.

The second point that my interaction with Eagle illustrates has to do with the power of listening to your own inner voice rather than the discord or gossip you may encounter in the outer world—after all, at the end of the day, you are here to live *your* life, to follow your dreams and make manifest your unique self-expression, in your career and in every other facet of your life. You do not have to allow yourself to be waylaid by the opinions of others, nor is it your responsibility to appease those who would much prefer you to prioritize *their* needs above your own. As the old saying goes, if half the people love you and half the people hate you, you're probably doing something right. In every case, the "right" thing is to follow your heart, even if this means marching to the beat of a different drummer. You might be surprised what you can create once you are committed to staying true to the rhythm of who you genuinely are.

Ellen DeGeneres, the Emmy-winning talk show host and one of my favorite luminaries and entertainers of all time, expressed this beautifully in her best-selling 2011 book *Seriously . . . I'm Kidding:* "Find out who you are and figure out what you believe in," she advises, "even if it's different from what your neighbors believe in and different from what your parents believe in. Stay true to yourself. Have your own opinion. Don't worry about what people say about you or think about you. Let the naysayers nay. They will eventually grow tired of naying."[11] Her willingness to maintain her authenticity in the face of opposition is an attribute that DeGeneres is beloved and admired for—especially since she accomplished it while standing on a global stage.

Today, making the decision to be open about one's homosexuality is commonplace, but back in 1997, when DeGeneres appeared—smiling and radiant—on the cover of *Time* magazine alongside the cover line, "Yep, I'm Gay," her coming-out was met with extreme opposition. Just a few months earlier, Ellen Morgan, the fictional character DeGeneres played in her hit sitcom *Ellen*, had made this same announcement, making DeGeneres the first openly gay lead actress to star in a prime-time TV sitcom. But despite the fact that the coming-out episode drew a landmark 42 million viewers, making it the highest-rated in the show's history, the network eventually buckled under the controversy, and a year later, *Ellen* was canceled.

Following the show's cancellation, Ellen described herself as having hit "rock bottom." She was out of money; she was uncertain if she would ever work again, and no one was returning her calls—but that, as they say, is history. Since making that pivotal choice to follow her authenticity, Ellen has gone on to host the Academy Awards, the Grammy Awards, and the Primetime Emmys. She is the author of four books and the founder of her own record company. She has won thirty Emmys, twenty People's Choice Awards, and numerous other awards for her charitable efforts. And, perhaps most significant of all, she has positively impacted the lives of countless people worldwide by upholding the message that it's okay to be exactly who you are. In an interview right before Ellen hosted her first Academy Awards show, Barbara Walters asked her about a skit that Ellen had performed on Johnny Carson's *Tonight Show*, in which she depicted a telephone conversation between herself and God. Barbara asked her, "If you were to call God today, what would you say to him?" "Thank you," was Ellen's reply.

> To chart our own course in any arena of life, we must give ourselves permission to listen first and foremost to ourselves.

As Ellen's remarkable story conveys, to chart our own course in any arena of life, we must give ourselves permission to listen first and foremost to ourselves. When we are living our own truth, not only are we incredibly attractive, but authenticity gives us the freedom to begin generating real momentum in the direction of our goals. So, how do you go about learning this skill?

Well, I can tell you that it isn't about ignoring everything that's going on around you or becoming insensitive to the needs of your boss, coworkers, or clients. It's about making sure you've prioritized your connection with your own internal guidance before seeking to connect with anyone or anything else. It's making the decision about how you want to show up and what emotional channel you are committed to resonating on before you ever walk through the door.

In the chapters that follow, we'll go into greater detail about exactly how to cultivate and maintain your own emotional and energetic environment apart from whatever environments you find yourself in, but to put it simply, it comes down to becoming responsible for your own point of focus and exercising your innate right to shift it on purpose.

Our Inalienable Rights

One of the most revolutionary ideals that was set forth in the United States Declaration of Independence is the principle that all people are created equal, and are "endowed by their Creator with certain inalienable Rights." Among these inborn rights are, of course, our right to "Life, Liberty and the pursuit of Happiness." And while the right to pursue happiness certainly includes having the freedom to own property and to acquire other forms of material wealth, I want to suggest that true happiness can only come about as the result of a decision that each of us must reach deep within ourselves.

Think about it: there is more wealth in the world now than at any time in history, but there also are more people living unhappy lives than ever before. The outer symbols of happiness that most of us have been encouraged to pursue—such as greater career success and more money—cannot actually guarantee our happiness, not only because they are dependent on changing conditions like the job market or the economy, but because not even the most ideal of conditions have the power to make us happy.

Most of us have been trained toward what I call an "outside-in" approach to happiness that goes something like this: After diagnosing some feeling of dissatisfaction or lack within ourselves, we identify the external acquisition that we believe will make us feel complete. "If only they'd give me that promotion," we decide, "then I'd feel appreciated at work." Or, "If only I made more money [or had a baby, or lost ten pounds, or had a second home where I can be near the water] . . . then I'd feel important." This fallacy in our thinking sets us on a lifelong journey toward an ever-shifting destination that we can never reach.

Anytime we look outside ourselves for an experience that can only be generated from within—such as approval, recognition, acceptance, or love—we are coming from a mind-set of lack, and as a result, nothing we ever do or create will be sufficient to fill that void. The new raise might initially put a skip in our step, until one day the novelty wears off, and we're back to feeling insufficient or underappreciated. Or, after working hard to attain the financial success we thought would finally earn us the respect we deserve, we are left with a feeling of "Is this all there is?" This is because happiness is a state of being that exists independent of external circumstances.

If you've ever known someone who managed to feel miserable or dissatisfied in the midst of what almost anyone else would perceive as an enjoyable circumstance, you already know that happiness can elude us in the best of times—and, conversely, that it is available even in the worst of times—because it is a choice we make on the inside. As psychiatrist and Holocaust survivor Viktor Frankl writes in *Man's Search for Meaning*, "Everything can be taken from a man but one thing: the last of the human freedoms—to choose one's attitude in any given set of circumstances, to choose one's own way." Frankl, who thrived despite living in the most degrading and horrific of conditions, understood fully that the happiness we seek begins with our innate ability to direct our minds and our focus in the direction of our own choosing, regardless of what is happening around us.

> Everything can be taken from a man but one thing: the last of the human freedoms—to choose one's attitude in any given set of circumstances, to choose one's own way.

Developing a Proclivity for Positivity

In the same way you can laser in on an interesting conversation that is taking place across a crowded room, you have the ability to direct the power of your focus to sift through the billions of pieces of data that come your way in every millisecond, and selectively choose to give your attention only to those that build your confidence, feed your passions, or forward your desired outcomes. With every thought you think and every emotion you offer toward your vision of creating quantum success in your career, you are forming a present-moment relationship between you and this future manifestation. And the quality of the attention you direct toward it will either encourage or discourage it to thrive. Knowing this, you can begin to use the power of your thoughts to your highest advantage.

In their 2007 book entitled *Creating Money*, Sanaya Roman and Duane Packer—two very gifted clairvoyants with whom I studied in the late 1990s—share their understanding of why positive thoughts have more creative power than negative thoughts. "One positive thought can cancel out hundreds of negative ones," they explain. "Your soul stops your lower and negative thoughts from becoming realities unless having them manifest will teach you something that will help you grow. You are loved and protected by your soul and the universe. As your thoughts become higher and more positive, your soul allows more and more of them to manifest. The more you evolve, the more power your thoughts have to create your reality, and the more responsibility you have to think in higher ways." As we explored in the previous chapter, there truly are no neutral thoughts, because every thought we offer evokes a corresponding emotion, and the collective energy of what we send out is always returned to us in the interactions and results we receive. On the surface, indulging in a chronic mental dialog such as "My talents are not valued," or "I work with a bunch of idiots," may seem innocent or even amusing. But from an energy standpoint, it is not. Like the constant litany of terror and tragedy that comes across the screen on the evening news, the dialogs we routinely engage in have the potential to tear us down—or, conversely, to build us up.

Creating the outrageously fun and successful career that you desire will require you to become more intentional about the mental and emotional "channels" you spend the majority of your time on. And just because the frequency you're currently tuned to reflects the habits of thought that you're most accustomed to—or those you inherited from your family or the culture in which you were raised—you are not doomed to watch this one channel for the rest of your life. With a little deliberate intent, you can change the presets on your emotional dial, and tune the receptors of your senses to home in on a whole different version of reality. By engaging your power of focus, you can filter through the infinite possibilities and grab hold of the ones you want.

By engaging your power of focus, you can filter through the infinite possibilities and grab hold of the ones you want.

Controlling Your Own Emotional Dial: Putting It into Action

Begin with the understanding that what you focus on expands, and *you* are the only one who has the power to direct your focus. By making a decision about what emotional channel you choose along the entire continuum of possible feeling states, and by consciously tuning yourself to that channel, you will alter your perception and therefore your reality. Anytime you realize that you don't like the channel you are currently watching in the area of your career, you have the ability to change it.

To change the channel of your most frequent thoughts and moods concerning your career:

- First, identify what channel you are currently on. As you examine your current situation, be open to discovering all the ways you are actually in alignment with the emotions of lack or longing or discontent in the area of your career or finances, and then allow yourself to put a name to that channel in order to distinguish it as something separate from yourself. Are you tuned to the Struggle channel? The Frustration channel? The Overwhelmed channel? What is the emotional or energetic essence of the channel you're tuned to currently?

- Now, realizing that there are countless other frequencies that you could *choose* to tune to, allow yourself to identify what channel you would prefer to be on. If you were living a career expression that you absolutely love, what would your experience be? Would you be tuned to the Financial Freedom and Abundance channel? Or the channel that broadcasts and receives purpose, passion, and quantum success? What is the emotional or energetic essence of quantum success as it pertains to your career?

• Next, just like in the 1970s, when we actually had to get up and walk across the room to change the TV channel so you could watch the show you wanted, put out your hand and physically act out the motion of changing your dial to the new channel of your choice. As you do, allow yourself to sense the vibration of this new channel. How does it feel to reside here? What are you now inspired to do differently from before? What new choices, ideas, and opportunities are available on this new wavelength?

• And finally, identify what new actions you can take to support the continuation of this higher frequency—and take them.

4

CONJURING THE ESSENCE OF QUANTUM SUCCESS

"Use whatever excuse you can to vibrate in harmony with those things you've been saying you want. And when you do, those things that are a vibrational equivalent flow into your experience in abundance. Not because you deserve it, not because you've earned it, but because it's the natural consequence of the Law of Attraction. That which is like unto itself is drawn."

—THE TEACHINGS OF ABRAHAM-HICKS

BENEATH YOUR DESIRE TO MOLD YOUR CAREER to conform to a specific image or to produce a specific result, there is a deeper desire to *feel* a particular way as you express yourself in this area of your life. This is true of any desire, big or small, that arises in any part of your life—whether it's to remodel your home, meet your soul mate, or get your body back in shape. On the surface, these might seem like common enough goals that are worth pursuing for their own sake, but look deeper and you'll discover that the reason you want to create

any of them is because you believe that in having them, you will feel
better in some way. To uncover the deeper feelings that are driving
your desire to create quantum success in your career, you need only
ask yourself, "Why do I want this?" and "What is the feeling I believe
I will experience in the having of it?"

For example, it was a feeling of absolute freedom that I was seeking
when I left my job as a pharmaceutical sales trainer to start coaching
people full-time. I did not want to be limited to a certain number of
vacation days per year, nor did I did want to be capped in how much
money I earned or had the potential to earn. Most of all, I wanted my
career to be an avenue through which I could explore the deep calling
within me that was urging me to grow, evolve, and expand my understanding of who I am and what I was born to do. I wanted the work that
I did to be inspired from within, versus motivated by a need to please
someone else—which is exactly what I have now created. I am so passionate about my work that I will often work on a Saturday afternoon
after my boys' karate class, not because I have to, but because I love it so
much and am inspired to.

When I listened to that inner calling to pursue my passion for
coaching others, I was ready to free myself from the person I had been,
and intuitively sensed that changing careers would be the most direct
and fruitful path to this new level of self-discovery. And at each stage
along the evolution of my career, the experience of freedom is exactly
what I have continued to nourish and create.

I now have the ability to structure my schedule in a way that
supports my career as well as my lifestyle. Almost everything I do
takes place over the Internet, so I can work at whatever time of day
or night I'm inspired to, and from anywhere in the world. I have an
amazing staff, whom I call my Dream Team, that is made up of a
huge array of fabulous people, all of whom have unique and diverse
skill sets that support me in doing only those things that I truly love

to do. My business is profitable, lucrative, abundant, and continuing to expand. And the more connected I remain to the essence of the freedom that I am seeking, the more of this experience I attract into my reality.

To try this on in your own life, bring to mind the vision of the success you desire in the area of your career, and go past the outer appearances of what you want to create, to the inner feelings you believe that creation will bring you. If you desire success because you believe it is an avenue for earning more money, for example, go deeper to uncover the feeling that you believe the money will bring. You're probably not drawn to having more money because you like the way it looks, or because you enjoy the feeling of paper between your fingers. It's more likely that you want greater financial prosperity because you are longing to experience a deep, essential feeling that you believe will be yours in the having of that. It might be a feeling of worthiness, of empowerment, of self-love, or of freedom, just to name a few.

The desire for more money may be nearly universal, but the feelings that drive this desire are unique to each one of us. This underlying feeling is what I call the *essence* of your desire. No matter what you want to create in the outer world, what you are really seeking is the feeling of this internal essence. Learning to attune yourself—in thought, emotion, and energy—with the essence of what you want to manifest, *while it is still in its unmanifested form*, is the key to attracting it, in living color, into your "real" life. To get a sense of the emotional essence that you believe you will experience once you've created your ideal career, try the following exercise:

> Learning to attune yourself—in thought, emotion, and energy—
> with the essence of what you want to manifest, *while it is still in its*
> *unmanifested form*, is the key to attracting it, in living color, into
> your "real" life.

CONJURING THE ESSENCE OF QUANTUM SUCCESS

Bring to mind a vision of you—happy, prosperous, and at the top of your game in relation to your career—and see if you can identify the deeper needs and desires that would be satisfied if this vision were right now your current reality. What would you have more of or less of if this vision were already fulfilled? Would you have more security, more freedom from worry, a simpler life? Do you imagine yourself being able to say no to activities you don't want to do, no longer feeling plagued by certain problems, or having the freedom to do what you want with your time? To the best that you are able, imagine yourself living in these new cir-cumstances; then, with a deep breath, allow yourself to go even deeper. If this were your reality, what higher qualities or feelings do you believe you would have greater access to? Would you experience more inner peace, more love, self-esteem, satisfaction, or happiness?

Now, having identified that deeper need or desire, ask yourself what you could do right now, in your present circumstances, to begin to bring more of that feeling into your life. For example, feeling and ex-pressing love for myself is an integral part of my vision, and my weekly massages and acupuncture treatments are two actions that I regularly take to foster this feeling.

If you're not sure what activities would support you in cultivating your essence feeling, simply begin making a list of everything you can possibly think of doing that would be consistent with that value. If *joy* is one of your essence qualities, ask yourself, "What activities bring me the feeling of joy?" Write down whatever comes to mind, from the mundane to the outlandish. Paring your vision down to its feeling essence is the most efficient way to take back your creative power, because regardless of your circumstance, there are always actions you can take to bring more joy, or freedom, or satisfaction into your life.

I hope you have begun to accept what mystics, scientists, and physicists have known for a long time—that everything that is now manifested as a visible, tangible reality began as an invisible energy that could not be seen, heard, smelled, tasted, or touched. If so, then I have some important questions for you to consider: Right now, in this moment, where exactly is the visible, tangible career success that you're longing to experience? Where is that thriving online empire that you desire to create? Where are the big royalty checks that you envision will one day be rolling in? If everything is in fact created twice—first in the mind and then in reality—then where does the process of creation really begin? The answer to these questions is that the success you desire already exists right here, right now, in the invisible but no less real realm of energy. This is the birthplace of every manifestation.

The energy of the career success you desire exists at the very core of you, as the essence of all you came forth in this lifetime to be, do, and express. It is a culmination of all that makes you uniquely you, and the sum total of all the wisdom you have gained as a result of your life's experience—wisdom that you deeply desire to pass on in some way and form for the benefit of your fellow human beings. The essence of your career success need not be created, because you were born knowing it at the deepest level of your being. And until it is fully actualized in the particular way that you envision it, you will not be completely satisfied. If you are to succeed in calling it into a full three-dimensional, external reality that you and all those around you can observe, you will need to locate it first within yourself, within the subtle realm of your thoughts, dreams, desires, and emotions.

I can't tell you how many times I envisioned in my mind's eye the car I wanted to drive, only to one day realize that I was now driving it. Or how many years I affirmed to myself that I had become a *New York Times* best-selling author before that accomplishment was finally achieved. Long before I ever met my husband, Frederic, I envisioned myself posing for family pictures with a loving husband and two kids—

and although in my vision it was a girl and a boy (the universe knew better than I did on that one), the essence of my desire unfolded nonetheless. The idea here is that you must nourish your inner vision with as much love, creativity, and intention as you imagine one day applying to the manifestation that has been created.

If I were to ask you right now to look for tangible evidence of the success you desire in your already-manifested life of form and phenomenon . . . to rush right out to your mailbox to count the number of checks you've received, or to Google your name to see if the world has recognized you as the Internet mogul you desire to be . . . well, I'd hate to be the one to break it to you, but you would not find it there—not yet, anyway. In this chapter, I am going to guide you into a new paradigm of creating success that will probably fly in the face of everything you've previously been taught. But to realize the full manifestation of the success you're looking for, you must learn to focus the power of your mind and emotions to tune in to the plane of existence—to the specific energetic channel—where the essence of that success already exists.

Waiting vs. Having

In the manifestation of any desire—whether it's a desire to become a major league pitcher or the desire for a peanut butter sandwich—there is always a lapse of time between the moment we realize we want it and the moment we throw that first pitch or take the first bite. But what is it that determines how long that period of time lasts? Why do some people seem to manifest their desires quickly and seamlessly, while others work on the same goals for years with little to show for their efforts? The answer to this question—and the key to more quickly realizing your goals—lies in understanding the difference between dwelling in an attitude of *waiting* and stepping into the attitude of *having*.

The key to more quickly realizing your goals lies in understanding the difference between dwelling in an attitude of *waiting* and stepping into the attitude of *having*.

If we're really honest with ourselves, most of us would have to admit that we've been waiting for that ever-elusive "one day" to arrive, when our wishes have come true and our daily lives reflect the ideals we hold in our hearts. We might be waiting for our soul mate to appear, for that big promotion, or for the day when the house is paid off, the kids are in college, and the retirement fund is complete. "When that happens," we tell ourselves, "*then* I will really feel successful." In my work as a life coach, I have met so many people who think that if only they had more influence, more money, more fame, more *something*, this outcome would lead them to the feeling of success they desire. But what I can tell you for sure is that this is a trick, an optical illusion that will sidetrack you, if you allow it, from realizing all the possibilities for success that exist right in this present moment, for an empty promise of "someday" success that lives somewhere out there in the future.

Now, I don't mean to imply that there is anything whatsoever wrong with striving toward the next experience or the next accomplishment; in fact, the desire to become more is a beautiful part of life and essential to the process of our evolution, and is one of my favorite aspects of being a human. But if we deprive ourselves of happiness and satisfaction along the way, pretending that the success we desire will be ours only when we reach some future destination, we trap ourselves in an endless cycle of wanting and waiting that prevents us from ever reaching the promised land of finally *having*. More importantly, as long as we are waiting for a particular outcome to occur in order to feel happy or successful, we deprive ourselves of the experience of loving the life we have *right now*. And the secret to getting more of anything you want is to love and appreciate what you already have. To decide that you are less satisfied than you wish—or feel less fulfilled or less successful—in the circumstances you find yourself in right now, is to come from a worldview of lack and an attitude focused on what's missing. And you simply cannot create abundance from a place of lack, ever. It defies universal laws. As long as the powerful lens of your focus is directed primarily on what's missing, you blind yourself to the very resources that can take you where you want to go, and what's missing is all you can see.

What Are You Waiting For?

By uncovering the future outcomes you've been waiting for (perhaps unconsciously) in order to finally feel successful, and deciphering the feelings you think those outcomes will provide, you will shift your focus from one of *waiting* to one of already *having*, and speed the rate at which all your desires manifest. The following statements may help you to discover how you might be holding the career success you desire as a future experience that you're hoping will happen "one day," rather than as an experience that is accessible in this, and every, moment. As you read each one, notice which scenarios resonate for you:

I'll feel really successful when I . . .

- Get promoted

- Have a certain number of clients

- Get my degree

- Pay off my student loans

- Make X dollars per year

- Achieve a balance between work and my personal life

- Can pay for my kids' college

- Earn the recognition I deserve

- Am in a position to retire

- Write a book

- Don't have to work so hard

- Am regarded as the best in my field

- Have a passive income stream

- Get out of debt

- Become famous

Now, for each of the above statements that applied to you, take a moment to ask yourself, "How do I think I will feel once I attain this outcome?" The answer to this question will reveal the essence of what you truly desire. For example, if you think you will feel successful once you finally write your book, I challenge you to look deeper. What is it that you're hoping to experience—on a feeling level—once you've achieved this goal? Will you feel relieved? Important? Validated? Understood?

Likewise, if your definition of career success includes receiving the respect or recognition of your colleagues, you can break this down by asking yourself, "How will I feel when I've earned the praise and admiration I feel I deserve?" and listening for the internal feelings you are truly seeking as a result of fulfilling this external objective. I can tell you from personal experience that there is nothing inherently rewarding about being the object of another's admiration. But before you have this experience firsthand, it sure seems like winning over your critics or receiving the appreciation or respect of those you serve would provide some satisfaction. To get to the feeling essence of this, you want to dissect exactly what that satisfaction would mean to you: maybe you believe you'll derive a feeling of worth, or a sense of your own importance. Whatever it is, identify it and own it as the real juice you are thirsty for, rather than the external manifestation.

How will I feel when I've earned the praise and admiration I feel I deserve?

Whether your "one day" outcome is to become the CFO of the company you now work for or to make a million dollars as the owner of your own lucrative business, you'll get to the essence of this desire by asking the same question: "How do I think I will feel once this goal is attained?" And then, in order to bring this "someday" outcome you're hoping for into the present moment, you must become willing to generate within yourself, right now, the exact feelings you believe you'll experience once this goal is realized. There are two primary ways of going about this:

Appreciate What You Have by *Appreciating* What You Have

The word *appreciate* is so interesting, in that it offers two distinct definitions that allow us to understand its broader significance. In an everyday sense, to appreciate is defined as "to be thankful or show gratitude for." But ask an accountant or a venture capitalist the meaning of the word, and they will explain that appreciation is "an increase in the value of an asset over time." The fastest way to allow into your life more of what you desire—both in the form of the feeling essence that you're really after, and in terms of the material possessions that you believe will deliver that feeling—is to go out of your way to appreciate what you already have. In our constant striving toward the proverbial top of the mountain, it's so easy to lose sight of how much terrain we've already covered, and how far we've come in the process. To appreciate is to deliberately decide to stop, turn around, and take in the broad view that is all around you rather than focus only on the single track that lies ahead.

I had a moment like this recently, when the song "Independent Women" by the band Destiny's Child came on the radio. Having grown up watching my mom feel as though she didn't have many options because my dad was the breadwinner, I had decided early on that I would make my own money and never rely on a man to provide for me. In my early thirties, this song was like an anthem to me that continually brought me back to my commitment to this vision that I had conceived so early in life. On this particular day as I was driving alone in my car, I once again heard these lyrics:

> 'Cause I depend on me if I want it
> I depend on me.

Hearing this song again, a huge wave of appreciation washed over me, and I was able to see that everything I had envisioned for myself all those years ago was now a reality I was living. It is from this state of appreciating what we already have that we open up a portal for the universe to continue giving us things to appreciate. To quote the teachings of Abraham-Hicks, "The perfect creative stance is satisfaction where I am and eagerness for more."[12]

Look around your life right as it exists at this moment, and you are certain to discover countless realities that you are now living that were once nebulous "one day" goals. The house you are living in, perhaps; the relationships with the people in your life; even the career expression you are now living was once something that existed only as an idea or a far-out dream. There are so many aspects of yourself and your life that are already going amazingly well—and most of these sustain themselves with absolutely no effort on your part. The fact that you have plenty of air to breathe, water to drink, and food to eat—is cause for appreciation. That you live in some proximity to nature's beauty and were born with five distinct senses that allow you to receive it—is cause for appreciation. That you are a unique individual, here with a unique purpose—and that you are passionately interested in your own process of self-discovery—is cause for appreciation.

The energy of appreciation is one of the most attractive in all the universe. When we are appreciated by another, we feel seen, safe, validated, and inspired to do, be, and give even more. But in appreciating someone or something else, we generate this same level of high-frequency emotion within ourselves, because we cannot appreciate our surroundings without bathing ourselves in their abundant energy. As Voltaire, the eighteenth-century French writer and historian, pointed out, "Appreciation is a wonderful thing: it makes what is excellent in others belong to us as well."

The energy of appreciation is one of the most attractive in all the universe.

If you study the list that follows, two things become clear: The first is that we access two entirely different versions of reality when we view life through the expansive perspective of appreciation versus when we are viewing it through the narrow lens of insufficiency. And the second thing is that it is entirely up to us to determine which reality we experience.

Seeing through the Lens of Appreciation vs. Looking for Lack

Honoring your worth and time vs. Not honoring your worth and time

Giving and receiving freely vs. Not giving or being open to receive

Opening your heart vs. Closing your heart

Expecting the best to happen vs. Worrying that the worst will happen

Coming from your heart vs. Getting into power struggles

Doing your best vs. Cutting corners

Wanting everyone to succeed; cooperating vs. Competing

Focusing on how you can serve others vs. Thinking only of what others will give you

Telling yourself why you can succeed vs. Telling yourself why you can't succeed

Coming from your integrity vs. Compromising your values and ideals

Being aware and paying attention vs. Operating on automatic

Applauding others' success vs. Feeling threatened by others' success

What you actively appreciate "increases in value over time." Go out of your way to notice abundance in any one sliver of life and appreciate it when you find it, and you will open the doors of your own perception to realize more and more.

In relation to your career in particular, what if you were to stop to really appreciate the journey you have taken thus far, to reflect on where you started and on the many winding turns along the way? How many challenges have you overcome, and how many latent skills have you developed in the process? What if you were to appreciate the many evolutions of your own desire, and the refinement of your own preferences? And perhaps most important of all, what if you could appreciate all that you can't see now, because it is still in the process of unfolding? This leads us to the next powerful way to cultivate within you the feeling of already having achieved the quantum career success you desire. I call it "feeling forward." Learning to appreciate not just what you have already manifested, but all that is even now in the process of unfolding, represents a quantum leap in consciousness in which you become free of the circumstances that now appear to bind you, and gain instant access to your ability to create the future you desire.

> **To unleash your full creative potential, you need to focus forward, beyond what currently is, and toward the reality that is in the process of coming into being.**

Feeling Forward

When you lovingly give your energy and positive attention to what is in the process of becoming—in the same way a farmer tends his freshly planted crop or a newly pregnant woman joyfully anticipates the baby she will one day hold in her arms—you are actually training your mind to reach beyond the circumstances you are currently living to generate the feeling state of the essence of your desire. And on the other hand, if at any point in time you tunnel your focus to include only the reality that has already assembled around you—the exact number of dollars in your bank account, for example, or the number of clients you've served to date—you are limiting the astounding creative power of your thoughts and emotions. To unleash your full creative potential, you need to focus forward, beyond what currently is, and toward the reality that is in the process of coming into being.

HOW TO "FEEL FORWARD"

Focus your attention on an objective or outcome that you would like to create into being. For this exercise, it's important to pick something that you believe is possible for you to have, that you think positively about it, and that you approach this process with the intent to create it. Be as specific as you can about the higher quality that you believe the having of it will make available to you, and imagine and feel this higher quality being magnetized into your life as you contemplate it. See how many of your five senses you can recruit toward this end. What does the realization of your objective look like, sound like, and taste like? Use your senses to expand and enhance the feeling within you of already living this reality, because connecting to the feeling state is the most important part of this exercise. The best results come from playing with the sensations and pictures, and being creative and inventive.

Once you have located this feeling state within you, use your imagination to sustain the feeling for a minimum of sixty-eight seconds. Do this several times throughout each day, knowing that there are no "right" or "wrong" ways to go about achieving it, and that with practice you will naturally become more skilled.

As you contemplate the emotional essence of each of the outcomes that you associate with your wildest vision of career success, your work is to conjure with as much color and intensity as possible the sensation of this outcome having already been achieved. Imagine this future fulfillment in all its glorious detail. Seat yourself in your new office; position yourself at the podium on your book tour; feel the sensation of freedom and accomplishment as you appreciate the number of zeros on your bank statement. In your mind and in your gut, play with the feeling of having fulfilled every one of your career goals until this vibration is deeply familiar to you. Turn to the thought as frequently as you punch the preset button of your favorite radio station when you get into your car. And visit this channel often until it becomes the most popular one on your dial.

The ultimate test of your newfound ability to choose your own channel—and in so doing, regain control over your own mood—will arise when you are met with frequencies that clash with your own. We live in a world of incredible variety, and among millions of other people who are making drastically different choices about how they direct their thoughts and where they invest their energies. The more attuned you become to your own emotional guidance system, the more sensitive you will be when you encounter a particular person or situation that introduces static to your chosen frequency. And sometimes, the static we encounter is our own.

For as much experience as I have had in creating success, I still have moments when something will trigger old feelings of lack or limitation—and when that happens, my business reflects it, because, as it does with everyone, the universe is always responding to me and delivering either more of what I want or more of what I don't want, based on the energy that I give out. The way we interact with the energy of a desire that has not yet manifested determines whether we will allow it or disallow it to manifest into our lives. When we are focused on its absence, it remains in the unseen world and out of our reach. But by focusing on the presence of what is wanted—by imagining it, by looking for evidence of it, and by appreciating all the ways in which we already have it—we attract to ourselves more of the same.

> By focusing on the presence of what is wanted—by imagining it, by looking for evidence of it, and by appreciating all the ways in which we already have it—we attract to ourselves more of the same.

The Law of Sufficiency and Abundance

No matter who you are, where you grew up, or what your current situation is, you are—and always have been—abundant. You are already an abundant being, because you were born into an abundant universe where there is no shortage of resources. Look anywhere in the natural world around you and this will prove itself to you in an endless variety of ways: There are more than 200 billion stars in the Milky Way galaxy, which is just one in hundreds of millions of galaxies. There is enough water in the world's oceans combined that if you poured it over the United States, it would cover the entire land ninety miles deep. In the next sixty seconds alone, the sun will generate enough solar power to fulfill the energy needs of our entire planet for a year. The concept of lack is entirely man-made; nowhere in nature do we find evidence of it. Abundance is our original state of being, and the abundance I am referring to encompasses far more than material possessions or luxuries. Satisfaction, fulfillment, joy, ease, happiness, creativity, compassion, freedom, love, and well-being . . . these are all expressions of the essential, internal energy of abundance, and there is absolutely no limit to how much of this energy can be experienced, or by how many.

Most people are experiencing abundance, but rather than enjoying an abundance of freedom and happiness, they are creating an abundance of struggle, heartache, debt, or pain. The powerful Law of Attraction will magnetize to us the external conditions that are in alignment with our internal state of being, and so, as deliberate creators, the choice is really up to each one of us whether we want to attract an abundance of all good things, or an abundance of lack. You have the power to create it any way you want it. Ultimately, you create your life based on what you believe you deserve.

You create your life based on what you believe you deserve.

So what to do when you find yourself smack-dab in a mind-set of lack or limitation? Just realize that anyplace in your life where you are experiencing struggle, frustration, disappointment, or discontent, you are aligning yourself with some belief in scarcity. All there is to do is remind yourself of your decision to remain tuned to your own "essence" channel and that there is no limit to the abundance available to you or to anyone, and to challenge yourself to take on a more generous viewpoint. Your goal is to maintain so clear a focus that no other influences—internal or external—can pull you off track. As you become practiced at consistently offering the frequency of the essence of your desires, you will open up a bandwidth for new ideas, impulses, and inspirations to flow in that were simply not accessible to you previously. To the extent that you are able (and we'll talk more about this in a later chapter), anytime you are faced with an energy that isn't wanted, just keep turning your attention to the energetic frequency that you *do* want to foster.

Your work is to fall in love with the sensation of each of your desired outcomes having already been realized by you, and to allow these feelings—organically and in their own time—to inspire new ideas within you. And as each new thought is born of this new vibration, relish it, celebrate it, muse over it, ponder it, pretend it, and imagine it inasmuch as it gives you joy to do so. Turn more of your attention to what is in the process of becoming than what has already become.

Your work is to fall in love with the sensation of each of your desired outcomes having already been realized by you, and to allow these feelings—organically and in their own time—to inspire new ideas within you.

Initially, at least, it does require more mental effort to keep turning your attention to a reality that no one around you is currently able to observe, and yet this skill is the hallmark of every human being whom we've ever revered as a visionary or a true master. When Walt Disney, determined to make the first animated full-length feature film, approached entertainment executives, they undoubtedly thought he was crazy, calling the idea "Disney's Folly." Only much later, after *Snow White and the Seven Dwarfs* received an Academy Award and earned more than $8 million dollars (the equivalent of about $130 million today) was the true genius of his vision widely understood. In more recent times, Elon Musk, the founder of the automotive company Tesla and the creator of PayPal, is currently developing reusable rockets, as well as a futuristic solar-powered hyperloop transportation system that would ferry passengers from Los Angeles to San Francisco in about half an hour, traveling just under the speed of sound. Just imagine for a moment if that idea had been floated even twenty years ago!

What we call genius is nothing more than having the faith and the willingness to hold true to your vision, even in the face of naysayers who will invariably try to talk you "back to reality." A visionary sees in his mind or feels with her gut what has not yet been created—and in so doing, creates it—from the inside out. This is the work of being a deliberate creator: to favor imagination over cold, hard facts, and to lean more in the direction of possibility than reality. This is the only way to create truly extraordinary results. In the words of philosopher and poet

Ralph Waldo Emerson, "Do not go where the path may lead, go instead where there is no path and leave a trail."

Conjuring the Essence of Quantum Success: Putting It into Action

To connect with the essence of the success you desire, first call to mind the specific image of what you want your career to look and feel like, or the specific results you wish to create.

Once you are present to *what* you want to create, begin to ponder the question "Why do I want to create this?" What do you think the fulfillment of this desire will enable you to do, and in what ways do you think it will change the kind of person you consider yourself to be?

Next, allow yourself to imagine this desire as if it were already fulfilled, until you connect to the bottom-line feeling or energy that you want to experience from it. What quality do you hope having this career, accomplishment, goal, sum of money, or thing will enable you to experience or express? Is it joy? Abundance? Freedom? Love? Perhaps it's a feeling of accomplishment or pride, or maybe it's the contentment of resting at the end of each day, knowing that you've shared your time and energy in a way that enhanced the quality of another person's life.

Whatever the essence of your desire, notice in what aspects of your life you are already experiencing it, and identify what you could do for yourself that would enhance and expand your experience of it even further. Make a list of all of the ways you could experience this quality right now. Are there alternative ways for you to experience the essence of your desire? What actions could you take that would provide this?

As you take these actions, allow yourself to connect with this quality at an emotional level: Feel its essence in your heart. Feel it in your belly. Allow the vibration of this energy to permeate your entire body and radiate out through every cell of your being. And from this new frequency that is in perfect alignment with the essence of the quantum success you desire, allow yourself to become aware of any new choices or actions you are inspired to take—and fill yourself up with the energy of this new frequency as you are in the process of taking them.

When you're connected to the underlying energy you are seeking through the creative avenue of your career, this energy feeds you, refuels you, and inspires you—not at some future time when the destination has been reached, but at every step along the way.

5

LIVING INTO YOUR FUTURE

"You can't connect the dots looking forward; you can only connect them looking backward. So you have to trust that the dots will somehow connect in your future. You have to trust in something—your gut, destiny, life, karma, whatever. This approach has never let me down, and it's made all the difference in my life."

—STEVE JOBS

EXPLORE THE INNER WORKINGS of any victory of human spirit—whether it's a personal victory such as breaking the four-minute mile, or an achievement as astounding as those of Thomas Edison or Walt Disney, whose contributions uplifted all of humanity—and you will discover one factor that is common to all: triumph over adversity. The fulfillment of any vision, great or small, demands that we find a way to rise above the forces that oppose it, and, as Einstein suggested, to find the solution to the problems we face on a different level of thinking than the level of thinking that created them.

Most people define adversity as something or someone that exists outside of themselves whose intention runs contrary to their own, such as a competitor attempting to control market share, or a group of people resisting forward progress because it threatens them in some way. But I want to suggest that the most formidable form of adversity is something much more subtle than either of these examples. In fact, it is so pervasive that, like air to birds and water to fish, it is woven into our most fundamental perception of life. And for this reason, it is almost impossible to recognize this form of adversity for the real obstacle that it poses. In the same way that "good" is the enemy of "great," your highest vision of career success must overcome one powerful enemy in order to become fully realized. That enemy is the status quo.

The Latin phrase *status quo* is defined as "the state of affairs that exists at any particular time, especially in contrast to a different possible state of affairs." In this case, the state of affairs I am referring to is all that you have created in your career expression up to date; it's what you do and how you feel day in and day out. It's the "what already is" reality that can be quantified by looking at the current circumstances that surround you: the number of dollars presently in your checking account; the number of clients you now serve; the level of enthusiasm and creativity you experience while you are working; the ease or difficulty with which you create the results that you achieve.

Now, in truth, there really is no "status quo," in the sense that every moment provides a brand-new opportunity to approach our lives in a completely different way and to therefore create an entirely different range of results. However, by virtue of the attention we give to the current conditions in which we find ourselves, we not only unwittingly encourage them to remain the same, but we actually perpetuate the continuation of those very conditions into our future. Before we go further, let me give you a really tangible example of how this is so.

In truth, there is no "status quo," in the sense that every moment provides a brand-new opportunity to approach our lives in a com-had of him was what I had given her. She accepted, and we spent the rest of the session visualizing David as a competent, valuable member of her team who contributed positively to the company's success. Back at the office, when Jodi focused on looking for the good in David, and when she took the time to make sure that her thoughts, words, and gestures to him were supportive and encouraging of his success, she offered an entirely different quality of leadership to which David responded in kind. It took only a couple of weeks of practicing this new momentum before Jodi experienced David as one of the most cooperative members of her team.

So, in this situation, what was it that made the difference? Did David have a sudden epiphany that caused him to relate to Jodi in a more respectful way? No. Jodi overcame the gravity of her own past way of thinking; the gravity of her previously held beliefs; the gravity of the story she had been telling herself as a result of her past experiences with David. And in so doing, she broke through her own limitations and into an entirely different reality that was previously unavailable to her.

I'd like you to consider that the status quo you are now living—especially in the arena of your career—is functioning exactly like a gravitational force that is made up of all of the experiences, conclusions, and stories you have come to believe and to expect as a result of everything you have lived in the past. Your habitual actions, your most familiar patterns of thought, and the mood or attitude that you most consistently offer when you go to work or think about your ideal career all have an energetic or vibrational momentum to them. When you think, do, and conclude the same things (much of which is unconscious) over and over, day after day, deep grooves are formed within the brain's neural pathways. And like traveling on a well-worn road, the more practiced you become in these habits of thought and perception, the easier they are to perpetuate. Unless you disrupt this momentum and replace it with a different one, it will continue.

In order to create a future that is more, better, and different than

pletely different way and to therefore create an entirely dif
range of results.

I once coached a client (I'll call her Jodi) who came to
after having been promoted to a management position within
pany where she had worked for more than ten years. Her new
ruffled the feathers of some of her former colleagues, and she w
a hard time being as effective as she felt she had the potential to
new management role. There was one employee in particula
with whom Jodi consistently had trouble. In her view, David
against even her most diplomatic suggestions, and at times re
follow her directives at all. The first few sessions of our coachi
tionship were centered on Jodi's perception of how uncooperativ
was, and how powerless she felt to do anything to change his be
What Jodi did not know was that, at that same time, I w
coaching another manager at her company, one who also regula
teracted with David—and whose experience of working with hi
entirely different than what Jodi described. Gently, I suggested t
that by giving the majority of her attention to all the ways David re
her or the things he did poorly, the only parts of him she was able t
tice were the qualities that irritated her and reinforced her low opi
of him. As I continued to educate her about the power of the La
Attraction, she began to see that, truly, what she focused on was ex
what she was attracting.

I explained to Jodi that in this case, there were two fundam
tal paths stretched out before her: she could perpetuate the mom
tum of the status quo by continuing to see David as an uncooperat
employee—and in so doing, continue finding evidence to support th
belief—or she could accept responsibility for seeing him in an entire
different light.

I invited Jodi to pretend that the following day in the office woul
be her very first time meeting David, and that the only knowledge sh

anything you have lived in the past, you will have to overcome the drag of this gravitational force in the same way that a spaceship must break out of the earth's atmosphere before it can move with any efficiency toward its destination. To do this, you will have to learn to give more attention—and therefore more credence—to the reality you desire to create in the future than to the reality you are presently living. This chapter will equip you with the techniques to do this, by teaching you how to step into what I call your "future self."

> Give more attention—and therefore more credence—to the reality you desire to create in the future than to the reality you are presently living.

Right now, there are actually thousands of possible futures that you *could* live into—in your career expression and in all other aspects of your life. Depending on the choices you make today, you could create a future career expression that you would experience as depressing and disempowering, and you could just as easily call into being a future that is awesome beyond anything you've ever imagined. In every moment— by virtue of the thoughts you think, the perspectives you hold, and the mood or feeling state you bring to each action you take—you are nourishing into existence one of two future realities. You are either creating the future experience of your ideal career, or you are creating the continuation of your current experience. It all comes down to which possibility you are using as a focal point of the majority of your attention.

Energy Flows Where Attention Goes

The phenomenon that we now define as the Law of Attraction is far from new. In fact, this universal law has been written about and passed down throughout the ages by countless teachers and wisdom traditions.

When Buddha made the observation that "As a man thinketh, so he becomes," he was conveying the essence of this powerful law. Even the Golden Rule, which advises us to "Do unto others as we would have others do unto us" is a testament to the basic understanding that what we put out eventually comes back. What you focus upon, you create a relationship with, and the quality of that relationship depends upon the quality of the attention you offer it. The act of focusing our present-moment attention upon a particular outcome—whether that outcome is something that is wanted or unwanted—generates a stream of creative energy that flows toward those eventual outcomes. Now, on the surface, this may seem like an obvious statement of fact, but the application of this principle is far more subtle than most people realize, because often we think we are nourishing the vision of a desired outcome with our positive energy and attention, when in actuality we are weakening and diminishing it with the energy of pessimism and doubt.

> **What you focus upon, you create a relationship with, and the quality of that relationship depends upon the quality of the attention you offer it.**

What is essential to realize is that it is not possible to flow positive and negative energy toward a vision at the same time. You are doing one or the other at any given moment. Just as you cannot dwell on a problem and simultaneously be receptive to its solution, you cannot move toward your desired future while your attention is fixated on a present that is less than satisfying. Like Jodi, most of us are blind to the ways in which, day in and day out, we choose the automatic continuation of the past over the deliberate creation of the future. And what's worse, we are unaware that our default way of perceiving the world is not through a wide-open lens of infinite possibilities, but through the incredibly limiting lens of what's already happened in the past. This is why those who have not yet learned the science of creating their lives on purpose seem to manifest the same predictable results—and the same predictable problems—time and time again.

If you keep telling the story of the past—particularly if it's a past that wasn't satisfying to you—you will perpetuate those same experiences and feelings. To create a future unlike anything you have previously known, you have to break free of the gravity of the past, generate a new momentum, and tell a new story. Simply put, you have to start telling the story of your success rather than lamenting the story of your failures.

Deconstructing Your Story

The stories we tell ourselves about ourselves—and in particular those about how much success is possible for us, how easy or difficult it is to achieve, and how much of a role factors such as education or social connections play—are not the truth. Like the story Jodi told me about David, our life stories are constructed at an unconscious level and are made up of the sum total of all of the experiences we've lived—the pleasurable as well as the painful—and the interpretations and beliefs about ourselves that we came to as a result.

A good portion of the stories we now tell about ourselves were passed on to us, both verbally and nonverbally, from parents, teachers, caregivers, and others who influenced us early in our lives. Long before we can even speak, we begin gathering information from those around us about what it means to be human, what it means to be a successful adult, and what is expected of us in order to be regarded as a productive member of society. And all of this information is imprinted upon us as the beliefs that we consciously or unconsciously hold.

Pay attention to those around you, and you'll begin to hear how each individual's personal narrative shapes every facet of their life—from their level of self-confidence, to the positions they judge themselves to be qualified or unqualified for, and ultimately to the amount of success they allow themselves to achieve. Without even realizing we are doing it, most of us recite the story of our past as a way of justifying or explaining the circumstances we currently find ourselves in.

For example, I recently worked with a client, Cindy, a city planner who opted to take an attractive position with a private firm in lieu of going on to earn her master's degree. Several years ago she discovered that this decision was preventing her from advancing any further in her chosen career. If in the four years since making this discovery Cindy had spent even five hours a week working toward her master's, she would easily have earned the degree; instead, she applied this energy toward justifying her earlier decision and explaining why the seemingly obvious solution is out of her reach. This is Cindy's story and she is sticking to it—year in and year out—even though it builds the case for why her career is stalling rather than encouraging it to thrive. In this way, the stories we tell ourselves about our past have a tremendous impact on how many possibilities we are able to realize in the present.

The human brain is made up of billions of neurons—and trillions of synapses—which use electrical and chemical messengers to carry information from one neuron to the next, allowing us to receive, interpret, and respond to all of the data arriving from the environment around us. According to an article published by the Urban Child Institute, a nonprofit organization dedicated to promoting the health of children, synapses are formed at a faster rate during the first three years than at any other time in a person's life. So, for example, if your parents were steeped in a mind-set of lack and limitation with regard to money, it's very likely that these beliefs were registered in your sponge-like little mind long before you understood that you have the power to question them. And once they are imprinted on these receptor sites, the messages they carry are transmitted at a cellular level far beneath the level of our conscious awareness. Here is a very short list of some of the beliefs that many of us inherited from our upbringing, beliefs that form the basis of the stories we now tell about ourselves:

- My destiny is predetermined.

- Hard work is the only path to success.

- My happiness is dependent on others' approval.

- My future will be a continuation of my past.

- Life is hard.

- Money is always a struggle.

- It's hard to make ends meet.

What's vital to understand is that anytime beliefs like those listed above (which only scratch the surface of all the possible variations) are allowed to persist unchallenged, they operate in the background of our consciousness—similar to a computer virus—coloring our perception of ourselves and others and influencing the direction of our thoughts, emotions, and behaviors. For example, a woman whose early life experiences caused her to create the belief *I'm unworthy*—perhaps as a result of being neglected or abandoned by a caregiver; enduring physical, emotional, or mental abuse; or even something as seemingly innocuous as being teased by other children at school—will, without even knowing it, make choices in every area of her life that are consistent with that belief. Unconsciously, she might settle for working for an employer who takes advantage of her, or for a romantic partner who is unavailable or in some other way doesn't meet her needs. If she tries to upgrade the choices she makes by addressing each of these areas of her life on the surface, it's unlikely she will be able to effect any long-term change. But if she releases the belief that gave rise to these choices and updates her perception of herself, her behavior will naturally begin to reflect this change, and she will begin to create a new story about the degree of fulfillment that is possible for her in each area of her life.

In my own experience, throughout my childhood I observed my mother's beliefs around money, and the way she reacted to anyone who had a lot of wealth. "Those people have *beaucoup bucks!*" she would often say, and the energy behind her words conveyed the meaning that because they had money, these were special people. My father, on the other hand, harshly judged those who had a lot of money and referred to them in far less glowing terms. The conflicting associations that I picked up on from a very early age about money and what it means to have it resulted in me experiencing what I now understand as the phenomenon of "split energy," otherwise known as talking out of both sides of your mouth.

When as a young adult I tried to formulate my own beliefs about financial abundance, I didn't know which parent to be loyal to. Should I accept my mom's open admiration of money and of those who had it, and therefore strive to be abundant in order to please her? Or was I better off adopting my dad's apparent disdain for money, and making sure I never ended up being one of "those" people, lest I lose his love? Until I uncovered and untangled this inner conflict, my relationship with money reflected the split in my energy. I made money easily, but also lost it easily, and would find myself swinging between the extremes of financial abundance and being deep in debt. Once I reconciled this split inside of me and deliberately scripted my own story about what it means to have money, I started making it *and* keeping it.

Like the money story I inherited from my parents, the stories we tell about ourselves and about how life works operate far below the surface of our conscious awareness; as a result, we are not even aware of the ways they are defining and limiting us. But anytime a lack-based emotion such as fear or insecurity surfaces, you can be certain that it is connected to a belief in limitation that you've bought into about yourself.

I remember one Saturday morning when, as I was getting my weekly massage, an overwhelming feeling of anxiety came over me seemingly out of the blue. Because I had been doing this work for quite some time, I knew that this emotion was an indicator of a hidden belief in lack that was hindering me in some way, so I decided to follow the feeling. As I closed my eyes and breathed deeply, I heard my own voice saying, *You have used up all of your success.* Connected to this very limited belief was the outdated notion that success is like a limited pie, and that I had already claimed my piece.

Compassionately, I imagined connecting with the part of me that was still holding on to this limiting perspective and reminded her that there is not one pie that all of us must share, but that each of us has access to an entire bakery. I soothed myself with the understanding that limits and lack are not real in this universe and that the broader part of me knows only abundance. By locating the story I had come to believe as the truth, I was able to identify it for the falsehood that I know it to be and shift myself back into the feeling and essence of abundance. I then conjured an image of myself in the future (a process I'll share with you in the next chapter), already living the success and abundance I desired for the next phase of my life. I have never experienced that feeling of lack related to using up all my success again. In recognizing the story for what it was, it was transmuted.

Granted, I've been doing transformational work for twenty years and have become practiced at shifting perspectives on a dime. If you are new to the idea that you can change your reality by changing the story you tell yourself, the following step-by-step exercise will guide you through the process of transforming any unconscious stories you may be telling yourself about why you cannot create the abundance you seek.

STEPPING OUT OF LACK-BASED STORIES

Reflect on a desire you hold related to creating greater abundance in your life and career, and notice any lack-based emotions—such as anxiety, frustration, resignation, or fear—that are triggered when you bring this desire to mind. It's not essential to label or pinpoint the exact emotion you are feeling; it's only necessary to identify whether, in relation to this desire, you are feeling good or bad. Bad-feeling emotions indicate that you are coming from a perspective of lack, while good-feeling emotions reflect a state of abundance, receptivity, and positive expectation. As lack-based feelings surface while you contemplate your desire for greater abundance, allow yourself to fully feel the emotion, and to notice in which locations in your body this feeling seems to reside.

Then, understanding that all emotions reflect the free-flow or stagnation of energy, and that energy is always in a state of motion, give yourself permission to move the lower, slower energy of lack to a higher frequency of abundance. As you will discover when you experiment with the meditation that follows, you can use your breath to locate the parts of your body that are holding on to a perspective of lack, and then imagine that—like a dam that is no longer able to hold back the pressure of water that wants to flow—the energy of lack is being released from your body and mind. Take as much time as you need to experience this release.

You can also visualize your limiting thoughts as words written on a chalkboard—"I'm not smart enough to earn abundantly," or "I have used up all of my success"—and then imagine erasing them and writing on the chalkboard in their place, "I have unlimited success available to me at all times." Another useful tool is to imagine any of your lack-based thoughts or emotions moving into a bubble of light and then watching them dissolve and be replaced with more abundant thoughts and beliefs.

It's important to keep in mind that anytime you set an intention to create something more in your life, whatever is standing in the way of you having it will naturally come to the surface. These are simple tools you can use to rewrite the story you consistently tell yourself in relation to abundance, and it's a skill that becomes easier and easier the more often you do it.

Our story—who we think we are, the experiences we've lived, where our family came from, what we have deemed to be our strengths and weaknesses, and what we have identified as being possible and impossible for us to achieve—keeps us rooted in a reality that has already manifested. To put it bluntly, it's old news. To create beyond anything you have created before, you will have to learn to tell the story of who you are, where you've been, and where you are currently headed, not in the way it has been, but in the way that you now want it to be.

> **You will have to learn to tell the story of who you are, where you've been, and where you are currently headed, not in the way it has been, but in the way that you now want it to be.**

Forward Thinking

If you consider the advice I just offered in a different context, you'll see that it's not the stuff of far-out fantasy, but actually a way of relating to life that you already employ in certain situations. For example, imagine that you are someone who is actively looking for a long-term relationship, and you are right in the middle of the most amazing first date with a man or woman who really interests you, inspires you, and lights you up. In this instance, the only "reality" that has already manifested is that you are sitting there with someone you've just met. You know very little about the facts of his or her life; you know very little about his or her history. So, if your mind is not busy cataloging the facts and details about "what is," what is your mind doing? It is dwelling in possibility. It is relishing every single aspect of the current interaction and conjuring thoughts, images, and feelings about the future. Is it a crappy future that your mind is envisioning? No, it's a brilliant, fulfilled, happy future. This is what I call "forward thinking."

Using our minds to conjure, imagine, and fantasize about the future comes completely naturally to us when we are children; you continue to do it when you're imagining a scenario of living happily ever after with someone you've just met, dreaming about the baby you will one day hold in your arms after learning that you are newly pregnant, or considering the possibilities in regard to a new position you've just accepted. Forward thinking is a state of positive expectation in which we don't concern ourselves with what is, but allow ourselves to lean—in body, mind, gut, and spirit—in the direction of what *could be*. It's allowing ourselves to daydream about the desired future; to talk to our friends about it; to imagine and fantasize about what will happen next. This may seem like fantasy or wishful thinking, but it is the stuff that creation is made of.

Most of the world believes that first you must attain the external prize—a better storefront, the big client, the coveted position—and once it's fully manifested, a feeling of joy, satisfaction, or excitement will be your reward. But again, I assert that the exact opposite is true: everything that we attain in the manifested world of form and phenomenon begins in the invisible world of intention, desire, and positive expectation. And these powerful invisible forces eventually gain enough momentum that they simply must manifest into a corresponding tangible reality. Freeing yourself from the previous ruts that narrowed your perception of what is possible is such an amazing process, because the space that used to be occupied by limitation and self-judgment becomes available for creating an entirely new possibility. You are literally opening up the space in your physical, mental, and energetic bodies for your future self to reside in.

Meeting Your Future Self

To get a sense of the power of forward thinking, allow yourself to recall an earlier time in your life when you were in the midst of some kind of challenge. Maybe it was a problem you were having with a boss, or a breakdown in a relationship with a family member or a friend; anytime in your life when you felt confused, blocked, or unsure about how to proceed. And now imagine that right now you had the ability to go back in time and transmit to that younger version of yourself all the experience, wisdom, confidence, and resourcefulness that you possess today. Can you see how much the younger version of you would benefit from your now wiser and broader perspective?

Just as the older, wiser person you are today would have a lot to offer that younger version of you, there is a part of you that I call your "future self" that is available to you in this moment. This aspect of you has already become all that you are now striving to be. It possesses an expanded awareness and a broader perspective, and is unlimited by the beliefs that have hindered you in the past. It knows that all things are possible and it has the ability to guide you in an infinite number of ways toward the outcomes you desire.

You already have a relationship with the abundance you desire. You have a relationship with the level of success you want to experience. You have a relationship with the adventure and fun and thrill that you want to magnetize into your life through the avenue of your career. The question to ask yourself is, "What is the quality of those relationships?"

The lower your vibration, the more you are resisting, and therefore hindering, the process. The higher your vibration when you contemplate the outcomes you desire, the more attractive you become to them, and the faster and more fluidly they manifest. As you develop an energetic relationship with this future self, you'll begin to glimpse visions of the person you want to be and the career you want to create—not as some far-out, dreamlike image, but as a reality that has already manifested in your future. You'll start to notice that the future you've envisioned is effortlessly informing your thoughts, your ideas, your feelings, and the range of possibilities that are available to you in the present. Just as you can bring the awareness you have today into the past, you can bring the expanded level of awareness of your future self into your present—and when you do, you will radically increase the rate at which your goals and desires manifest. I have so many cases in point of how this phenomenon has played out in my own life, even during the time when I was the most unhappy and least fulfilled.

> You already have a relationship with the abundance you desire. You have a relationship with the level of success you want to experience. You have a relationship with the adventure and fun and thrill that you want to magnetize into your life through the avenue of your career.

Before I learned that I could create my life on purpose rather than by default, I was living in a rented room in a small, ant-infested house with a very strange woman, because I was $60,000 in debt and could not afford to rent my own apartment. I had also just ended a relationship with another "bad" boy, and had put on a good twenty pounds after the breakup. It was in this period of strong discontent that I began asking for answers and deliberately seeking out clues to help get my life onto a different and more positive track. Each insight I received during this time led to the next, and after a year or so of consistently studying and applying the principles of manifestation that I've been sharing with you throughout this book, I received a vision of my future career success that was so big that I could hardly wrap my head around it at the time.

I was doing a meditation I'd learned in a course called Awakening Your Light Body, which I now offer through my coaching academy, and was using a technique for establishing a connection with my aura, or energy field, and using this connection to magnetize my desired experiences and outcomes into my life. During this particular meditation, I received an image of a book with my name on it—a book that had helped and inspired so many people that it had become a *New York Times* best-seller. I could actually feel the pages of the book turning . . . that's how real the vision was.

Now, at that time, this vision seemed completely out of my reach—after all, I hadn't even written my first book yet. This vision was a gift from my future self, and in the process of continuing to lean in the direction of my desired future and away from my troubled past, the reality of becoming a *New York Times* best-selling author did come to pass, *twice*.

I continued to nourish the vision of what I wanted to create in every area of my life: being financially free and living in a beautiful home of my own; feeling great in my body and being able to shop anywhere and wear beautiful clothes that I felt amazing in. I also set the intention to create a healthy, loving, conscious partnership with a man who was ready for a committed relationship.

I was committed to creating some major shifts in my life, so I studied and practiced these principles diligently. And over time, I began to have many experiences that confirmed that the quality of the energy we send out is reflected back to us in the quality of the energy we attract from those around us. The more I applied these laws, the more I felt things shift—both in the quality of the experiences I was creating in my life, and in how I felt about myself inside.

I remember one day in particular, after I had been working with this technology for exactly five years. I looked around my life and took an inventory of what I saw, and realized, *wow*! Everything I was now living was consistent with the future reality that I had envisioned five years earlier: I was living in a beautiful house with nice furniture, very similar to those I had always admired. I had a great-paying job. I was in a committed relationship with a man whom I would ultimately marry and stay with for eight years, and I was also back to a size 4, which is the ideal size for my body. It was one of those moments when I realized just how powerful this process is, and how important it is to defy the gravity of our current conditions and to create and nourish a vision of the future we want to live instead.

That day of realization was more than fifteen years ago, and I have continued to use these same tools to re-create my life time and time again. Even to this day, I am absolutely amazed each time I reach a new pinnacle in my career or accomplish a long-desired goal in my personal life that was once a future vision. I have had the déjà vu experience more times than I can count where I realize that I am standing in the present moment in the exact place that was once the subject of my future vision—whether it's looking out at the view from the Eiffel Tower, being interviewed on national TV, or manifesting a ticket to go to the Grammy Awards. This process works, and the manifestation—when it catches up with the vision we've created—is far more surprising and delicious than anything we can allow ourselves to envision ahead of time.

You see, it doesn't matter if your life right now is miserable or incredible; there is always another level of expression, empowerment, and creativity that is accessible to each one of us. When you begin to direct the majority of your energy and attention toward the future you desire, rather than a past or a present reality that is less than satisfying, you will speed the rate at which you attract quantum success into your life.

There is always another level of expression, empowerment, and creativity that is accessible to each one of us.

Adjust Your Wavelength

Your future self exists as a wavelength—a particular frequency that you are naturally attracted to because it represents you, as the full expression of all your potential. This frequency is constantly on the lookout for an open channel to broadcast itself through. If you hold the intention that everywhere you go and everyone you interact with is a potential channel through which that part of you can manifest, this is exactly what you will find. In practical terms, being open to the wavelength of your future self requires that you change the normal filters through which you usually perceive life.

For example, when you receive invitations to participate in activities, don't listen to them through your normal filters, such as "How long is this going to take? How much is it going to cost? What's in it for me?" These are all examples of the filters that most of us use when interacting with opportunities and other people, and they keep us focused on what already is, rather than on what could become. Instead, listen to every opportunity that comes your way as a potential avenue through which you can connect with the quantum success you desire to create in your career, and trust your intuition when you get the impulse that something is a match.

When I first started coaching, I used to teach courses through the Learning Annex because it provided an avenue to meet other like-minded speakers, make new business contacts, and attract coaching clients. Back then, I had a website that was up and running and fully functional, but was not producing any business for me. I also had only a scant 750 people in my online community, and the robust online community of nearly a quarter million people that I now adore was nonexistent.

While traveling to a conference, I began to envision a future that included someone to tend to the virtual side of my business. I pictured someone creative, easygoing, great at what they do, and a blast to work with. I was having so much fun just envisioning this! I felt the relief of being able to delegate tasks that I wasn't interested in doing or didn't fully understand. I felt the excitement of creating a bigger funnel that would allow me to reach more people. I imagined the exhilaration of filling more courses and empowering more people. . . . In fact, I spent the majority of the three-hour drive to the conference that day engrossed in this vision, and by the time I arrived at the first session, I had enlivened it with so much energy and emotion that this new member of my fledgling business felt like a reality to me.

Later that day, I was introduced to Jon, who had built a thriving online business for his mother, who now had an online community of more than 120,000 people. Excitedly, I introduced myself to him and expressed interest in working together. He replied that his calendar was so full that it would be at least three months before he could even have a phone conversation with me, but I did not let that deter me, nor did I let that present reality talk me out of the feeling of recognition that came over me when we met. Instead, I asked him to give me a date to follow up with him, and told him that I was anticipating a long and successful working relationship together. I left the conference, excited to have made the connection, and went on about business as usual: writing, hosting a radio show, speaking at colleges and Learning Annex events, and leading one-on-one and group coaching programs.

Three months later, I followed up with him—first by e-mail and later by phone—and the rest, as they say, is history. Jon and I worked together for more than ten years, creating wildly successful launches for my programs and having a blast doing it. Even if I had hired a recruiter to scout the entire nation, I could not imagine finding anyone smarter, more creative, or more fun to work with than Jon; he was absolutely perfect for what my business needed to grow at that time—and I literally bumped right into him after conjuring this image of my future self with the right support.

This is how effortlessly meetings and opportunities unfold once you have taken the time to envision—and to energetically, emotionally connect with —your future self. Not only do you draw the right people and resources into your experience; more importantly, you're able to recognize them when they show up and have the confidence to pursue them even when there appears to be an initial obstacle. Because you've already practiced the vibration of this ideal future, it feels like the next logical step when it begins to unfold in your experience.

Imagine, Connect, and Expect

Creating a present-moment, real-time relationship with your future self is a three-part process that begins with allowing yourself to *imagine*. This part of the process is about letting yourself dream as big and as freely as you can so you can begin to conjure an image of the most awesome, fulfilling, successful career that you are able to conceive of right now. It's important to underline here that your ideal career might be completely different from anyone else's image, and that is perfect! This is all about you and what you truly desire. So just see if you can release any notions imparted by your family, industry, or society about the kind of work you should do, and release the limitations of what you're currently doing or how much success you've created in the past. Take some time to let your imagination wander, until you begin to laser in on what it is that you would like to create for yourself in this area of your life.

You want to visualize and imagine a future in which you are engaged in work that feels powerful, purposeful, and prosperous. Ask your future self to show you images of what your day-to-day life looks like. How many hours a day do you work? How much freedom and flexibility do you have in your days? How big of an impact are you making on those around you—whether it's on animals that you work with, or on the people you work with, or in pursuits that you engage in on your own?

Allow yourself to remember and to connect with what you are truly passionate about; to think about things you would love to do regardless of whether you got paid to do them. This is the *imagine* part of deliberately creating quantum success in your career, and it's important to have this image as clear as possible before we move to the next step, which is to energetically *connect* with that vision.

Connecting to your vision is about deliberately accessing the feeling state of already having fulfilled it. It is to become energetically aligned with the vision of you working in your ideal job, or running your ideal company, or performing the work that you already love with more clarity and efficiency, and to allow the energy of your thoughts, beliefs, moods, and actions to become one with that vision.

As you are connecting with this vision of your ideal career, see if you can identify the essence of how it feels. What does it feel like to do work that really comes from the heart, that you are passionate about, and to which money flows naturally and abundantly? In your awesome, ideal career, do you feel more powerful, more productive, more fulfilled? Be as descriptive and detailed as possible as you reach for this feeling essence, and feel yourself connecting on an emotional and energetic level with this reality. Does it feel like freedom, or complete well-being? Is it joy, success, abundance? Maybe it's an experience of feeling content and fulfilled at the end of each day. At this point in the process you are just looking to uncover "What is the feeling that I want to experience?"

The third and final step is to *expect* that the shifts you desire to make—in this case, in your career—are already in the process of unfolding. Expecting is really about believing: believing that it's possible; believing you are capable of creating it; and believing that you are deserving of having it.

At this point, you want to become conscious of what your current expectations are in relation to creating an abundance of career success. Do you believe there are limitations to what you can create—and if so, what are those beliefs? As you identify the thoughts or beliefs you feel are preventing you from trusting that what you want is within your reach, just know that your future self is not limited by any of those; that there is another, broader perspective available from which you can relate to your career, and that your future self already holds this perspective. Continue to conjure the image of you showing up in your career at your absolute best, in a state of financial freedom and well-being, and notice the thoughts and feelings that surface in response.

These are all beautiful glimpses of the gifts your future self holds for you in the area of your career—because this is the pure energy that you are at your essence. Each day as you continue to connect with this image and with the feelings, thoughts, ideas, and inspirations it generates, imagine that you are connected to your future self by a beautiful line of light energy, almost like a baby connected to its mother in the womb. Your future self is constantly feeding you nourishment, resources, and ideas that will help to bring your vision into full bloom. It is transmitting energy to you all day, every day, like a lifeline. You have complete access to this future reality, because you have a relationship with the larger, broader part of you.

The more you establish an energetic connection with the future self that has already created your most ideal career, the more intimately related you will become with this aspect of yourself. No matter what your specific career goals, connecting with your future self will accelerate the unfolding of them. For example, if you're seeking to be promoted within your company, energetically create a relationship with the "you" that has already received that promotion. *Grow into it*, mentally, emotionally, and energetically. Consider how it would feel to have already earned it. What changes would it inspire within you? Would you walk, speak, dress, or carry yourself differently? Would it effect a change in the way you relate to your coworkers? Whatever shifts you can foresee yourself making, step into them now. In order for any relationship to grow, you have to feed and nourish it. And the way you nourish your relationship with your future self is through your attention, your imagination, and your energy.

If you think for a moment about someone in your life who is extremely important to you—your child, for example, or a parent, or your spouse—what you will discover is that you actually carry a part of their energy with you wherever you go. The connection is always there—regardless of whether you're in each other's presence or thousands of miles apart. Your connection with this person is so strong as a result of all of the time, attention, intention, and energy you have already invested in your relationship with them. You've nourished this connection with your attention and energy; you spend time contemplating your relationship with the person even when you are apart; you've imagined your future together; you've recalled positive feelings that you've shared in the past and anticipated more positive experiences in the future . . . and all of this has contributed to the strong bond that you now have with this person.

This is exactly the kind of relationship you want to keep creating and strengthening with your ideal career. You want the energy and essence of that future self to become so dominant within you that your present awareness has no choice but to entrain with this energy and allow the momentum of it to build. When you find your attention drawn off track by something in the present that is inconsistent with your future self, take a moment to envision that part of you the way you would like it to be. Remember, what we call "reality" is in a constant, never-ending process of becoming. The most abundant, clear-minded, successful version of you already exists! You've connected to it and invited it to enhance your experience. Now it's just a matter of shortening the distance between you, and you do this by continuing to bring it into your awareness in a way that feels good when you do it.

What we call "reality" is in a constant, never-ending process of becoming.

Living Into Your Future: Putting It into Action

Begin by acknowledging that there are actually thousands of possible futures that you *could* live into in relation to your career expression, and that in every moment—by virtue of the thoughts you think, the perspectives you hold, and the mood or feeling state you bring to each situation and interaction—you are either calling into existence a future career expression that you would love, or you are creating the continuation of your current experience. It all comes down to which possibility you are using as a focal point of the majority of your attention.

Make the decision to adopt the art of "feeling forward" as a daily practice. Begin by noticing all the ways you are currently giving more attention to the status quo than to what you want to create, and then making a list of at least three aspects of your career that would be more beneficial to focus on instead. How would you rather perceive this situation?

Imagine that the story you've previously told about your career—complete with its ups and downs, wins and setbacks, and colorful cast of both villains and heroes—has perfectly prepared you for the future that is now in the process of unfolding. How does this story end? Write or speak about the details of your future self, about all the life experiences that provided wisdom and insight, and about the quantum success that you are now in the process of manifesting.

6

CREATING THE CLIMATE FOR QUANTUM SUCCESS

"You only have control over three things in your life. The thoughts
you think, the images you visualize, and the action you take."

—JACK CANFIELD

THROUGHOUT THIS BOOK, it has been my intention to upend many
of the outworn and inaccurate perceptions that foster a disempowering and dissatisfying experience of your career, in order to ground you
in a firm, personal understanding that you have the power to create
whatever experiences you desire. We've dismantled the superstition of
materialism and explored how energy is both the basis of and the pre-
cursor to everything that eventually manifests into what we perceive
through our physical senses. We've overturned the notion that other
people, places, or things have the power to "make us feel" a certain
way, and embraced the understanding that raising the vibrational frequency of our current emotional state is as simple as changing the
channel on a TV. We've seen how we can transform our experience

in any aspect of life by deliberately raising the energetic frequency of our most dominant thoughts, feelings, and actions. And we've learned to no longer allow the present "reality" that is playing out before us in real time to dictate our mood or attitude, and to focus instead on the unfolding of the version of ourselves and our future that we most desire to live.

There are two additional, essential tools that will make your tool chest as a deliberate creator complete: The first is an understanding of the role that contrasting and no-longer-good-feeling experiences play in the creation of what you *do* want to create. The second—which we will explore at length in this chapter—is the knowledge that, just like a radio station or news channel that broadcasts a certain genre of information to its audience, you have the ability to control the content, tone, and quality of the energy that you surround yourself with, no matter what environment you find yourself in. The Venerable Fulton John Sheen expressed this beautifully, saying, "Each of us makes his own weather, determines the color of the skies in the emotional universe which he inhabits." Not only do you have the ability to create your own weather, you have the power to mold the forecast to your own personal preference.

Long before others know anything about you, or make the decision to hire you for a position or to bring you into an important project, they have already begun to gather essential information about you on a subtle or vibrational level. On the surface, they are of course making assessments about the way you are dressed and the words you choose when you speak; but, energetically speaking, there is much more going on in every encounter than meets the eye.

On an energetic level, we are always feeling out those around us and noting both consciously and unconsciously whether we're naturally drawn to them or repelled, and sensing whether there is resonance between us. If you've ever been in a conversation with someone and were not able to focus on their words because you were preoccupied by something that just didn't *feel* right about the speaker, then you know firsthand what I'm talking about. The mood or energy we carry with us—which others pick up on via eye contact, voice inflection, body language, and basic "gut feelings"—is an all-powerful communicator. To paraphrase Ralph Waldo Emerson, "Who you are speaks so loudly, I can't hear what you're saying." The essence of who you are is registered by everyone you come into contact with, in the same way your senses register the temperature, wind current, and humidity of the climate when you walk outside.

The more deliberate you are about the way you present yourself, the more others will get who you are at a more subtle and powerful level than can be conveyed with words. As Jack Canfield, one of my earliest mentors, once pointed out, "You can't become a $10,000-a-day keynote speaker if everything about you is consistent with a speaker who earns $1,000 a day." By consciously creating a climate of success around you, you will naturally evoke a different perception—and therefore a different level of participation—from everyone you interact with.

Hand in hand with creating a clear vision of your successful future career is creating an environment around you that invites, encourages, and nurtures that ongoing success. The people in our lives—including our friends and family as well as our colleagues and business associates—are continually reflecting back to us the same degree of impeccability that we demonstrate through our attitudes and actions alike. Through the power of our example, we teach those around us how to treat us and set a precedent that everyone in our environment responds to.

Through the power of our example, we teach those around us how to treat us and set a precedent that everyone in our environment responds to.

The Warm-Up

Think about some of the intricate rituals that professional sports teams perform to ready themselves before taking the field for a season-defining game: dancing, turning backflips, forming into a circle and jumping in unison—even hitting themselves and their fellow teammates in preparation for the battle that's to come—and you'll begin to get a sense of what it means to "warm up" before an important event. At this point in the game-day countdown, the coach's motivational speech is over; there is no more mental preparation to be done, no more rehearsing the first play. In that moment, the only thing left to be accomplished lies in the realm of emotion and vibration, as each teammate creates his or her own personal environment of victory before ever stepping foot on the field. Can you imagine an effective pregame ritual that was otherwise? What if the players took those crucial twenty minutes before starting time to mentally rehearse all their past mistakes, to recall exactly how it feels to drop a pass or miss the clutch shot? It would be ridiculous to deliberately cultivate an environment of failure at the very moment you want most to succeed, right? Yet this is precisely what many of us do unwittingly when we allow our energy to become split by wanting an outcome and doubting our ability to create it at the same time. To be at the top of your game, you need to bring yourself mentally, emotionally, physically, and spiritually into complete *alignment* with the outcome you intend to create. Without this essential inner preparation, any external action you take may very well end up creating momentum in the wrong direction.

Every external manifestation of success—whether it's a sports team that has gained the winning edge, a business idea that is taking off, or an ad campaign that's gone viral—is characterized by an internal state of alignment. Some people refer to this as the state of being "on fire" or "in the flow"; others attribute it to being guided by a divine purpose or a higher calling. Regardless of the words you use to describe it, when you tap into the free-flowing, high-vibrating energy that is complete internal alignment, you feel invincible and unstoppable, and all of your actions (and even your thoughts) yield incredible results. Think back to Michael Jordan circa 1985, making 3-point shot after 3-point shot and joining Wilt Chamberlain as the only two professional basketball players to score 3,000 points in a single season. People often attribute this kind of success to hard work, luck, or being the recipient of an extraordinary amount of support, but in truth, none of these conditions have anything to do with it. In fact, success on this scale cannot be forced at all; the only way to attain it is to allow it.

Ambition and effort certainly have a role to play in the manifestation of any type of success, but, contrary to what most of us have been taught, they represent only a small part of the equation. To create true *quantum* success—which is success that brings us contentment and fulfillment rather than overwhelm and stress—we have to learn to balance the masculine energy of pushing forward with the feminine energy of yielding and allowing. The universal Law of Allowing is based on the understanding that creation is just as much a by-product of the inward ebb as it is of the outward flow. Just think about it: the tide first has to recede in order to gather the strength to form into a wave. A seed must first be buried deep into dark soil before it receives the impulse to begin its upward journey toward the sun. There is no such thing as "goal setting" in nature. Trees don't strive to reach a certain height. Air doesn't work to be drawn to and consumed by fire. Planet earth doesn't clock in each day for another shift of orbiting the sun. So how does this universe function, then, if not by hard work and willpower? It functions through the simultaneous phenomenon of attraction and allowing. In the same way that plants are attracted to light and planets are magnetically pulled toward the sun, every human being has the power to magnetize into our lives all that we desire. And this power hinges on how much we are able to *allow*.

In the process of working toward any goal, it's important to remind ourselves that striving, controlling, and forcing do not have the power to bring us what we really want, because anything achieved through those means will demand a sacrifice of intimacy, connection, and balance. We might achieve the goal, but at the cost of taxing an important relationship or even our own health. By becoming more allowing, we become more receptive to the replenishing energies of relaxation, surrender, and peace. And once our internal alignment is stable, every action we take in the direction of our desired outcome will result in positive, forward momentum.

> Once internal alignment is stable, every action taken in the direction of our desired outcome will result in positive, forward momentum.

The Exponential Power of Alignment and Momentum

Most of us are accustomed to hearing the word *momentum* as it relates to sports. We understand that a team described as having momentum is on a roll and will be difficult to beat. But momentum is actually the principle behind Newton's first law of physics, which states that an object at rest is more likely to remain so, while an object in motion tends to stay in motion. Momentum is the force or speed produced by anything that is in motion. This applies to physical objects, such as a boulder rolling down a hill, and it applies equally to the motion forward (or backward!) of our most practiced thoughts, feelings, moods, habits, and behaviors.

When a project, idea, or enterprise has gathered enough momentum, it quite literally takes on a life of its own. What type of life that entity will take on depends upon how aligned we are internally while we are in the process of manifesting it in the physical world. It is the degree of alignment or misalignment in our energy that determines whether our actions generate upward momentum or downward spirals—and whether we are met with open doors and green lights or detours and dead ends.

Now, I realize this philosophy flies directly in the face of what most of us were taught—and there are certainly plenty of successful people who would disagree. Just a couple of weeks ago, I ran across this quote from Estée Lauder, perhaps once the richest self-made women in the world: "I never dreamed about success," she said. "I worked for it." I certainly understand this philosophy, and deeply respect it. In my own career, I've done it both ways. I've worked hard and pushed forward beyond what felt comfortable, motivated by the desire to reach a goal or to prove my worth, to make money, to make my mom and dad proud—and I accomplished all of those things. But it was not enjoyable, because I was driven to achieve, rather than inspired to action.

I know firsthand about the anxiety that comes along with using action to force something to happen before it's ready, and the physical burnout that results from using up energy that I did not have in order to create an external result. This extrinsic, action-only approach is the culprit that drives our addictions to caffeine and other stimulants and can ultimately lead to adrenal burnout. Action alone is like using an electronic device that is relying on battery power alone, whereas action that is fueled by inspiration is like using one that is plugged in and being fully charged by a live electrical current.

In the early years of my career, this battery-powered approach was my go-to way of operating, and—like most people—I didn't even realize that it was possible to approach success any other way. But once I began practicing and applying the universal laws that are at work behind the scenes in every manifestation, I shifted my approach entirely, and began working with *aligning my energy* before taking any action. Now, you will have to find enough resonance in these words to apply them in your own life—because you truly cannot take anyone else's word for anything—but I can tell you from personal experience and from coaching hundreds of thousands of people that the result of becoming more deliberate about and internally aligned with what you ultimately want to accomplish creates far more fun, joyful, easy, flowing, abundant success than any physical action offered alone.

When I work with energy first, I am unstoppable, because the two aspects of myself—the inner and outer; the physical and the divine—are co-creating and aligned, and the results springing from this partnership are beyond anything my human mind could imagine. So, are there physical actions that need to take place? Yes, of course. In my business, I create visions, goals, and strategies; I continually create new programs to better serve my clients; I catch those planes, get on those stages, record those videos, and show up whenever and however it's necessary. But because I understand that the essence of why I am doing all of it is to feel free, joyful, and abundant and to contribute to the uplifting of others, I summon these energies first, and bring all parts of myself into alignment with them.

Alignment is an internal state of being in which our energy, ideas, and desires are allowed to flow freely, rather than being opposed by our own resistance. When we're aligned, we not only have access to the full range of our own resources; we're also receptive to the unlimited stream of consciousness and intelligence where all ideas, solutions, and creative impulses are born. Actions that are taken after we've deliberately fostered a personal environment of alignment yield results that are so radically disproportionate to the effort expended, that some may label them as miraculous. What cannot be seen through physical eyes is the energetic momentum that was already in place before the action was ever taken—the result of internal alignment.

> Alignment is an internal state of being in which our energy, ideas,
> and desires are allowed to flow freely, rather than being opposed
> by our own resistance.

The musician who writes a Grammy-winning song in minutes . . . the artist who sits down to doodle an idea and ends up creating a

masterpiece . . . the scientist who grasps a cutting-edge concept in a sudden flash of insight . . . even the extraordinary and "impossible" accounts we sometimes hear about such as a mother lifting a car to save her child or physically carrying someone twice her weight to safety—these are all easily grasped demonstrations of the power of alignment, and yet they are far more rare than they need to be. When you take the time to foster an environment within yourself that is energetically resonant with the end result you want to achieve before ever setting yourself to the task, you create results with almost no effort; and in fact, those who have witnessed these types of manifestation often describe them as flashes of insight, synchronicities, and "aha" moments that seem to come out of the blue. The creations born from this state of alignment are better described as the results of receiving or allowing a creative impulse to flow through us rather than attempting to create anything specific. I have experienced this type of effortless unfolding many times in my life. For example, the cover of the first book I ever wrote, *Perfect Pictures*, came to me in a meditation, and for seven nights in a row after receiving this vision, I was awakened at 1:05 in the morning by a stream of consciousness that would ultimately become the content of that book. Years later, while in Maui getting a massage, the complete outline for a new program came to me as a flash of insight.

I had taken my family, many members of my staff, and all of my top affiliates (online marketing partners) on a decadent retreat at the Four Seasons to celebrate a recent success. Generosity is a quality that I deliberately cultivate in every aspect of my business, so it is not uncommon for me to show appreciation for my colleagues and staff by taking them on such thank-you trips. I was sitting outside in the shade and getting a foot massage while listening to the sound of the waves crashing in the background, watching my kids and my husband laughing and playing together in the pool. It was truly my own little slice of heaven on earth. I was completely relaxed, and so appreciative of all of the manifestations of alignment and abundance all around me. I was definitely not think-

ing about work. In fact, I wasn't thinking about anything at all. And into my very quiet mind came an idea to create a Facebook program in which I would offer my followers the opportunity to participate in thirty days of live meditations with me.

From the moment the idea landed, it ignited excitement in me. At that very moment, my social media manager "happened" to walk by, and we began chatting about the possibilities. She saw the vision immediately, and soon we were off and running on a creative brainstorm that was building momentum by the moment. Two weeks later, we launched the program. Not only was it wildly popular and incredibly profitable, but I absolutely loved leading the meditations, and the people who participated reported daily about the amazing shifts, changes, and transformations they were experiencing in their lives as a result. Many of them shared that they had grown so much and created such drastically different results that they could no longer recognize themselves from when they'd started just weeks earlier. Many of them continued to sign up to participate with me month after month after month, and still do.

And just in case this sounds like a case of coincidence or luck, or a by-product of the beautiful surroundings I happened to be in when it happened, I want to share another experience that I had right on the heels of the first one, because it truly proves the role that internal alignment plays in the external results we ultimately create. Unlike the Facebook idea, which occurred to me spontaneously and seemingly out of the blue during a moment of complete ease and enjoyment, a very similar idea was presented to me while I was in a meeting with a marketing guru I had known for years, and with whom I had worked closely early in my career.

This consultant suggested that I create what is known as a "continuity program," which is a program that is offered every single month so that participants can take advantage of ongoing coaching training. He explained that by not making this level of training available, I was

"leaving money on the table." Now, money alone is never cause to motivate me, but because he also suggested that this program would provide a way of serving our community that our coaching academy was not currently offering, I began to consider it. I felt no internal excitement, but logically it made sense, and the man who offered this advice had a great reputation, so I decided to implement it and launched it to my community of more than 200,000 people all around the world.

Well, a grand total of one person signed up for the program! Not even in the earliest days of offering one-on-one coaching had I ever launched a program and received so little response. For me, this was such a clear sign, and instantly I knew why it had not succeeded: while both programs provided more or less the same service, the first had been inspired from within me and received as a creative impulse from the Divine, while the second had come from someone outside of myself whom I believed I "should" listen to because he is an authority.

"Shoulds" for me are an indication that we are holding on to lack and limitation. When we "should" on ourselves, we limit our options, and we are deciding something based on someone else's idea of what our lives are supposed to be like, instead of what we would actually love and feel good about. Because I was doing what I believed I "should" do, rather than what I was inspired to do, I was not lined up with the idea, nor connected to the energy of what I wanted to create in the implementation of it. As a result of these experiences and hundreds of others like them, I now know in every fiber of my being that every one of us has within us the innate ability to manifest dreams big and small with effortlessness and joy.

Those "big breaks" that we sometimes hear about and may think of as someone's star suddenly rising are often not the cause of their success at all. On the surface it may appear that they became an overnight sensation, but in almost every case they have been practicing their craft—and practicing the vibration of the type of success they desire—for many years. Eventually, when the momentum gains enough speed, the internal energy they've been cultivating finally manifests in an external form that all can see, but, as Oprah Winfrey noted, "Luck is preparation meeting opportunity. If you hadn't been prepared when the opportunity came along, you wouldn't have been 'lucky.'" Which for me means, there is no "lucky." Success, or the lack thereof, is all a demonstration of the Law of Attraction.

Creating your own personal environment of quantum success involves nothing more than deliberately shifting yourself into a state of internal alignment before you take whatever actions you believe will contribute to that success. And while this preparation takes place in the realm of energy and is therefore invisible and unquantifiable, I can tell you with absolute certainty from my own personal experience, and from coaching hundreds of thousands of others, that if you take this on and make it a part of your daily practice, you will give yourself an advantage that almost no one understands.

In business settings in particular, there is so much emphasis on external actions and outer appearance. We know that to be taken seriously we must look the part, so we go to great lengths to ensure that our clothing, hair, nails, and makeup convey the type and degree of professionalism we want to project. Now, just so you know, I am a huge fan of nice clothing, and enjoy the fact that my work requires me to get dressed to the nines from time to time. But the new worldview that we are rapidly moving into demands that we give at least as much attention to tending to our vibration as we do to our exterior, because our energy communicates the loudest of all.

There is no value in smiling over the top of misery or frustration, and there is no sense in taking action before the inspiration to do so arises, because the universe and all its inhabitants are not responding to our outer veneer. As I often tell my coaching clients, prioritize making your energy body as beautiful as possible. Like energies are drawn together, and you want to have a say about whom and what you are resonating—and therefore, rendezvousing—with. The exercise that follows offers a quick way to make sure your internal energy field is consistent with and in harmony with the external outcome you want to create. I recommend using it at the start of each day, before making an important phone call or going on a job interview, or when transitioning from one segment of your day to the next.

BEAUTIFYING YOUR ENERGY BODY

Begin by finding a comfortable position, either in a chair or on the floor, that you can easily maintain for five or ten minutes. If possible, aim to keep your spine straight in order to allow an unobstructed energy flow through your body. Close your eyes and begin breathing calmly and slowly, taking about three seconds to breathe in, and three seconds to breathe out. Do this a few times, until you feel yourself settling into the present moment.

As you continue to relax your body, feel yourself growing calm, tranquil, and serene. In your imagination, travel through your body, relaxing each part. Mentally relax your feet, legs, thighs, stomach, chest, arms, hands, shoulders, neck, head, and face. Let your jaw be slightly loose, and relax the muscles around your eyes. Just feel each part of your body let go, and notice that the more relaxed you become, the more space within you becomes open to receive.

With your next deep breath, begin to see, feel, and imagine the energetic body that is an extension of your physical body. Some traditions call this your aura; science refers to it as the electromagnetic field. Bring forth the intention to connect with this nonphysical extension of your physical body, which is so receptive and so impressionable to your thoughts, feelings, and intentions.

And now with your next breath, gently begin to contemplate the activity you are about to engage in, or the segment of your day you are about to transition into, and allow yourself to receive a few words that describe your optimal state of being to approach this situation. If you were at your very best in this encounter, how would you feel and present yourself? What internal environment would you carry with you into this interaction? Allow yourself to identify some emotional words—such as *peaceful, clear-minded, strong,* or *happy*—that describe your ideal internal state, and as you do, use your breath to infuse your energy body with the vibration of this energy.

Allow yourself to feel the glow of peace, well-being, strength, and clarity gaining momentum inside you, coursing through every part of your physical body, and emanating to and through your energy body or aura. Without struggling to make anything happen, play with just how far you can feel your energy body extend. Can you feel it extend to the person with whom you are about to meet? To the clients whose business you want to attract? Allow this extension of your highest intention to be easy and delicious, and to fill you up from the inside out.

As you get ready to bring your attention slowly back into the room you are in, acknowledge the shift in the way you feel. Notice if your thought are different; if any new ideas have landed in your sphere of awareness; or if you feel lighter or have greater clarity. Savor and enjoy the state of calmness and peace that you have just created within yourself, and know that all of your future actions and interactions will be infused with this state. When you are ready, gently open your eyes.

Tending to the physical alone—and this includes the actions we take in the physical world—can only get you so far, because our physicality represents only 4 percent of the human equation. More often than not, anything that we do in the exterior world that we approach without first establishing alignment within yields more confusion and frustration than clarity and fulfillment. This is the rat race that most people are caught within, particularly in relation to their careers. Thinking that we can offer enough action to make up for a lack of being aligned with our vision is a lot like trying to receive your e-mails without first connecting to the Internet. It's futile, and a lot of energy is wasted in the process.

I always say that physical action alone is like getting into your car, turning the key, and stepping on the gas. The car will gradually begin to move and you will start to head in the direction you desire. But when you do energy work in advance of and alongside physical actions, you take off as if you have a turbo booster. You get to where you want to go with more focus, with less effort and energy, and with a flow and joy far greater than what physical action alone can bring you. Once you acknowledge—as I hope you have done by now—that you are both physical and nonphysical, you begin to understand that your first priority is to connect to the broader, more expansive part of you by tending to your own internal environment. And when the sunny climate of alignment you've created around yourself is clear and stable, it will persist no matter how much doom and gloom you encounter from those around you. Let me give you another quick example:

In 2008, in the midst of the most serious financial crisis since the Second World War, my coaching academy was in a period of exponential growth and was more profitable than at any time up to that point. When the Great Recession began, triggered by the bursting of an $8 trillion housing bubble, I had just begun facilitating an intimate group of ten people through a coaching program focused on how to create abundance. As it happened, nine of those ten people had careers that were directly related to real estate—as realtors, mortgage brokers, and those who worked in construction, renovation, and interior design.

In the middle of a plummeting stock market, successful companies laying off employees by the thousands, and rampant housing foreclosures, every participant in the course gained new clients—*big* clients.

Even the one participant who worked as a hairstylist and was not affected by the housing market reported off-the-charts success. After taking my Abundance Principle Coaching Course—in which I outline some of the principles you are learning here—she attracted clients who weren't just coming to her for the usual cut and color, but for blowouts, extensions, and other high-end services. Despite the vibration of fear and panic that was literally filling the airwaves, these folks continued to create great income, make sales, and attract new business—all because they had experienced the power of tapping into the energy of abundance, and had practiced the daily skill of creating an environment of abundance around them.

> **When the sunny climate of alignment you've created around yourself is clear and stable, it will persist no matter how much doom and gloom you encounter from those around you.**

Until we have the awareness and the knowledge about how to prepare our internal environment deliberately, this powerful technique also works in reverse. Here's another quick case in point: one day, my family and I paid a first-time visit to a quaint little restaurant situated right on the water in an area of Montreal called Sainte-Anne-de-Bellevue, where we live for the warmer part of each year. I had just had some clients in town for a two-day retreat who had discovered this little place and raved about how great the food was and how pleasant the ambiance. Intrigued, we eagerly visited the restaurant—but were not compelled to ever go back, for the simple reason that the environment the owner had created was not conducive to the vibrations of abundance and appreciation that are at the heart of our family's values; it was instead an environment of competition and scarcity that we found repellent rather than attractive.

It had been an exceptionally rainy spring, and business—as the owner told us repeatedly throughout our meal—had been very slow. It had been raining on and off that day, but the skies were clear when a party of eight arrived, requesting a table outside so they could enjoy the fresh air. The large party asked the owner to dry off the table outside so they could be seated; instead of happily obliging, he threw what could only be described as a fit, and began complaining to us about these demanding customers. Instead of giving these eight people the best possible experience of his food and the best service he could, he made everyone's experience tense and unpleasant. This man was a master at creating an internal environment that was so strong that it could be felt by all who entered it; unfortunately, the environment he created was one that reinforced a mind-set of scarcity and an atmosphere of complaint, rather than of appreciation and ease.

We foster around us what we consistently give our attention to, which is why, in my business, I am always looking for ways to create an environment of abundance. After all, abundance in all things is what I teach and how I live, and a philosophy that resonates with what I deeply and passionately believe. And in those moments when I am off my game and don't feel aligned with abundance—because after all I am human and have my own programming that I still need to adjust from time to time—I return to the same principles and practices that I've been sharing with you throughout this book. I recommit to my intention to bring this climate with me wherever I go, rain or shine—both with the people I support and with the staff members who support me. I take the members of my team on exotic trips, give them beautiful gifts, and most importantly, frequently acknowledge them with words of genuine appreciation. This generosity is returned to me tenfold, both in the quality of the contribution they make to me, and in the level of attention that each member of the team gives to those we serve.

We foster around us what we consistently give our attention to.

It's What You Give

There is a fundamental principle that you must accept before you can successfully begin the practice of bringing your own weather to the picnic, so to speak, and this is the principle of taking complete personal responsibility. Now, in the discussions we've had so far about recognizing our inherent ability to direct our own thoughts and to therefore generate our own moods and outcomes, we've already addressed to some extent the topic of being responsible for our own energy, but there is a next-level dimension of personal responsibility that I want to introduce here. And again, this understanding requires a bit of a paradigm shift.

Most of us were trained to approach life—our careers, our relationships, even the events we participate in—from the standpoint of what each experience may have to offer us. When contemplating a potential job or line of work, our first considerations are often "What are the benefits?" or "How much does it pay?" When sizing up a potential life partner, most of us are looking to see what he or she will be able to provide for us in terms of love, attention, and lifestyle. But I want to suggest that this approach robs us of something incredibly valuable that we must reclaim in order to become the stewards of our own success in any area of life: ultimately, none of us has any control whatsoever over how much another person gives to us, but we can take absolute responsibility for how much we give to others.

In his book *Secrets of the Millionaire Mind*, businessman T. Harv Eker introduces an idea that he calls the Law of Income, explaining that "you will be paid in direct proportion to the value you deliver according to the marketplace."[13] Several years ago, when I studied with Harv, he helped me to understand that money is the natural consequence of solving the problems of others, and the more problems we can help people solve, the more money we will make.

You were born with a unique set of gifts that are distinct from those of anyone else on the planet, and when you discover these and begin sharing them generously and abundantly for the purpose of uplifting others, success in all forms—including financial reward—will be the natural result. If you can make the shift away from looking at what each client or project can give to you, and look instead from the perspective of what you can give, you will dramatically change your relationship to money. There are problems that you alone have the ability to solve. There are things that life has taught you that can lead you, like no other, immediately to the solutions you seek. There is a specificity in the type of impact that you long to make, and particular results that life has built up a desire within you to participate in creating. When you think about what it is that you are uniquely qualified to give and keep this in the forefront of your mind while engaging in any activity professionally or personally, the quality of your work will increase, and along with it the quantity of dollars that flow in response. Abundance begets more abundance.

There is a second important element to embrace in this next-level understanding of personal responsibility, and this speaks to the very core of our ability to choose. Of course we all know that we are responsible for our actions and for the words we speak—and, happily, people en masse are now waking up to the power of taking responsibility for the energy they send out and therefore attract. But few people realize that the most fundamental thing we are each responsible for is the way we focus our own perception. As a case in point, you can choose to perceive your often-negative boss as an obstacle to your success or the sole reason for your unhappiness at work, or you can choose to see him as providing exactly what you need to become the masterful creator you were born to be.

You are the one writing the story, and you have the power to cast the characters in your life in whatever roles you'd most like them to play. Just be aware, however, that if you cast your boss as the oppressor in your drama, you will have to act out the part of the oppressed. And if you cast her in the role of mentor or view her as a personal trainer whose job it is to make you stronger, you will open up a whole new range of possible experiences. Remember, there is no "is" in what currently is. All things are in a process of becoming, and what they become depends in large part on the way we choose, in every moment, to look at them. And here I'd like to say that, of course, when someone has been consistently rude to us, or has shown up for years in a way that makes it easy to justify our negative feelings about them or the situation, it is not easy to simply think a different thought about that person. If it were that easy, everyone would do it. That is why doing the inner work I've been advocating throughout this book is so crucial to your external success. Any resistance that is within us, is within *us*, and therefore we have both the power and the responsibility to change it. But it takes a willingness to let go of all the things that our minds cling to as a justification for why we feel the way we do, or as evidence to prove ourselves right. The bottom line is that we all have the ability to change the story we tell ourselves, and when we do, our lives will out-picture the inner changes we've made. Your outer world and everything that manifests in it is a reflection of your inner world, and if you want to affect the circumstance, you first must affect the cause. This is a universal law.

> **Your outer world and everything that manifests in it is a reflection of your inner world, and if you want to affect the circumstance, you first must affect the cause. This is a universal law.**

Of course, however you choose to perceive your boss, your coworkers, your clients, or your career as a whole, that perception must become more than a fleeting thought or an occasional observation; it must become a consistent practice—a deliberate "beating of the drum" of the emotional tone you want to perpetuate in that relationship, to borrow the phrase made popular by Abraham-Hicks. If you are really committed to casting yourself as victorious, successful, and abundant with regard to your career expression, this must become the dominant way you feel most times that you think about it. This will take practice at first, but eventually, just like the everyday drive to work that you could do with your eyes closed, the mental journey toward your career success will become such a familiar one that you'll find yourself going there on autopilot.

The key to success in the practice of maintaining your own environment is to do it consistently—and, importantly, to do it ahead of time. If you wait until Monday morning to begin practicing staying positive around your boss or to see him in his most positive light, your odds of failing are much greater, because you have not prepared the environment in advance for that perception to take root. But if you were to invest some of your leisure time in mentally reviewing his positive aspects, remembering times the two of you have worked well together, or making a list of the strengths and abilities you have gained as a result of your interactions with him, you will give yourself the benefit of all that positive traction before the workweek even begins. Positive thoughts will come more easily, and you'll be better able to sustain them even when he demonstrates a behavior that is contrary.

When I worked in corporate America, I encountered my fair share of people who routinely helped me to strengthen my ability to maintain an internal environment of alignment even in the face of contrast, so I understand firsthand how difficult it can be to sustain this intention in the heat of the moment when it is being tested. The key is to continually remind yourself that at the heart of every person, situation, or encounter that you perceive as something that you do not want lies the potential of experiencing what you do want instead. In the moment that my then-boss, whom we sales trainers used to refer to as "Hitler in a woman's body," presented an attitude or behavior that momentarily challenged the environment I was committed to maintaining within myself, I would grab a notepad from my purse and immediately begin writing down everything I could think of that I *did* want in a boss. For example, "I want a boss who is supportive and listens to me"; "I want a boss who celebrates my success with the same excitement as his or her own"; "I want a boss whose respect I genuinely want to earn and who I am inspired to do my best for." Using that moment of contrast to clarify all the qualities that I wanted to be different, I imagined having a new boss who was supportive, fun, easy, encouraging, and positive.

Once you've identified what it is you *do* want, based on the clarity of knowing what you don't want, the next step is to focus on what it would feel like to already be living in this new and upgraded reality. In relation to my former boss, I asked myself, "How would it feel to have the opportunity to work for someone who displayed all of the qualities I listed and more?" And, more importantly, "How would being in that person's presence affect the quality of my attitude, behavior, and the effort I am inspired to bring forth? How would I show up differently if this was my reality?" If you can discipline yourself to resist the temptation to give others the responsibility for your mood, and accept instead that everything in your current manifested reality is a reflection of the vibration that you are offering, and that you have the power to adjust it at will, in time every situation you find yourself in will reflect the environment you've taken the time to cultivate within yourself. Not because the people around you have changed (although that certainly happens as well), but because you've trained yourself to deliberately look for the best in them, and what you consistently look for, you will find evidence to support.

In order to begin the practice of consciously creating your own personal environment, you first need to decide what kind of environment you desire, and then arrange yourself internally in such a way that your mood and expectation are conducive to creating that outcome. So, for example, if your intent is to create an atmosphere of confidence or excitement surrounding a new product you're launching, take some time before you introduce it to others to mentally review the list of your product's attributes, recall all that inspired its creation, and generate a feeling of genuine excitement within yourself about all the possibilities it holds. All of these actions will help you to prepare your internal environment.

Before you give your next big presentation, or before sitting down for an important conversation with a colleague or a friend, decide in advance what it is you most want to convey, both with your words and with your energy. Clarify your intention—not just in terms of a specific outcome you hope to achieve, such as making a sale or reaching an agreement, but in terms of the overall vibe you want to create between you and your listener. When I was still in the corporate world and going from one great job to the next, before interviewing with a potential new manager I would visualize a line of light connecting my heart to his or hers. In doing this, I was priming both the energy and the outcome of the interview before our physical bodies ever were in the same space and time. Whether you are creating an internal climate of quantum success as it relates to your career as a whole or just to one upcoming interview or meeting, remember that taking the time to do this is not for anyone else's benefit except your own. Practice conjuring the image of others as being beneficial to you in some way, and watch in amazement as new evidence of that benefit shows itself to you.

> **Practice conjuring the image of others as being beneficial to you in some way, and watch in amazement as new evidence of that benefit shows itself to you.**

Now, I realize that as you begin to consider what it would really look like on a day-to-day basis to show up in your career with this degree of deliberate intent and impeccability about the quality of the energy you are sending forth, you might be feeling concerned that this practice will require far too much effort, and that living your life by default is much easier by comparison. This is a common and understandable concern, and it's important to address. The answer is, yes: becoming intentional about the quality and frequency of the energy you're choosing to emit in each situation and maintaining that frequency throughout the day does require a certain amount of intention, which is why—in the same way you would never take off on a road trip with a gas tank on "E"—you have to approach this practice with a full emotional cup.

Pouring from a Full Cup

How you are feeling in any given moment has *everything* to do with the way you will perceive your environment and all who are in it. If you're tired or feeling overwhelmed; if you're having the experience of being crunched for time; or if some unresolved issue in your personal life is clamoring for your attention, you will find it much more difficult to generate and maintain a positive environment around yourself. This is why I recommend that before you attempt it—before you even leave your home, in fact—you go about the process of filling your own emotional cup. You cannot give to others what you yourself have not received, and when you fill your cup, you generate an overflow of energy that can be used to nourish every area of your life and to provide greater resources in situations in which you've previously felt unresourceful.

Filling your emotional cup means caring for your well-being by doing things that relax you, inspire you, light you up, or otherwise make you happy. It could mean taking the time to enjoy a hot bath rather than rushing through a shower, or getting up from your desk periodically to walk outside and enjoy the fresh air. It could be treating yourself to a new suit that you know will make you feel amazing for an upcoming interview or a big meeting. Maybe it's taking a dance class or spending time in your garden. The particular activity you choose is not what's important; the enjoyment that you take from it is, and often the act of *not* engaging in any activity at all is the most pleasurable gift we can give ourselves. Anything you do that sends the internal message that you are deserving of your own time, your own attention, and your own love will fill your emotional cup.

Recently I had the pleasure of visiting the Wolf Connection, a sanctuary and wilderness retreat in Southern California that is dedicated to rescuing wolves and wolfdogs and empowering our youth. One day, as our group entered the habitat of one of the female wolves, she was initially friendly and even allowed us to touch her; then all of a sudden— even though nothing had happened to make her ill at ease, at least that was visible to us—she backed up and hid behind the trainer. The trainer explained a concept that most of us humans don't understand, and even those who do often find it hard to implement. "The wolf is just self-regulating," the trainer explained. "Either she found the moment to be frightening or too overwhelming, and so she naturally surrendered to her instinctive urge to take her own space." What was so interesting was that none of us harshly judged the wolf for taking the action that felt best to her—and she certainly did not seem to judge herself. She did not care about how anyone else might react to her taking her space. She simply decided, for whatever reason, that she needed a moment to self-regulate, and once she had given herself whatever it was that she needed, she then willingly came back to the group.

To fill up your own emotional cup, you have to learn how to self-regulate. This means being aware of when you need to take a quick break in order to regain your alignment. It's honoring the subtle presence of less-than-good feelings before they gain too much momentum, and taking whatever action will provide you some comfort and relief, without self-judgment and without concerning yourself with how others might feel about it.

Anytime you find yourself thinking thoughts that are bringing you down and creating a climate of overwhelm or discouragement rather than of empowerment and success, take this awareness as a signal to self-regulate. Decide that it's okay to give yourself a moment to close your eyes, breathe, and find a better-feeling thought; better yet, keep a running list of go-to activities that nourish you and turn to them whenever you need an energetic pick-me-up. If you're relatively new to the idea of deliberately adjusting your own energy field, experiment with the effect that certain music, foods, drinks, activities, and environments have on your mood until you find those that yield the greatest benefit Any actions you take in the outer world will be far more effective once you've tended to your internal climate.

Now, you can't change the preset on your dial by tuning to a new station just one time. And in the same way, tuning your experience of your career to the channel where your highest vision resides will not come about by only attending to it occasionally. You have to make the decision to deliberately turn to this channel—to vibrate on this energetic wave of consciousness, to make choices that support and encourage this frequency—and to return to the clarity of this frequency throughout the day whenever you feel a little static creeping in.

NURTURING YOUR INNER ENVIRONMENT:
FILLING YOUR OWN EMOTIONAL CUP

Begin with an acknowledgment that it is both your right and your responsibility to do whatever is necessary to feed your soul and to fill your emotional cup from the inside out. You cannot give to others what you have not first generated within yourself, so begin this exercise by giving yourself permission to take this time just for you and affirming that you are every bit as deserving of your own love and attention as any of the other people, projects, and things that you give your energy to on a daily basis.

Take a moment to reassure yourself that your world won't fall apart as a result of you withdrawing from it for a few timeless moments, and, in fact, you will be more present, more effective, and in a greater state of harmony with all of the components of your inner world as a result of having taken this time.

Start by sitting or lying in a comfortable position. Take in and release a few slow, deep breaths, and bring forth the intention of relaxing completely into this moment, so that you can receive the full benefit of this process. Feel your feet relaxing, and the muscles in your legs letting go. Let your thighs and hips relax, and the muscles along your back. Take a deep breath and consciously relax your jaw and the muscles around your eyes. Notice how your breathing changes and deepens the more you relax. Sink into the comfort you are providing yourself in this moment. Breathe into it.

With each breath you take, imagine that you are filling yourself with light. And as you breathe out, feel yourself releasing and letting go of anything that no longer serves you—old thoughts, limiting perceptions, judgments, resentments, non-serving beliefs. . . . Allow anything that is blocking your full ability to receive the love and light that you are to melt away and be released from your physical, mental, emotional, and energy body. Feel the space that opens up within you as you consciously let these things go.

With your next deep breath, imagine again that you are filling yourself and this newly opened space with light, with expansion, with the very real possibilities that are even now making their way into your experience. Consciously expand your beautiful energy body, affirming to yourself that you and your life are unlimited; that you are an unlimited, abundant being. Feel yourself expanding into more and more of your potential and your inherent beauty and light. Allow yourself to receive even more of the unlimited abundance of this universe.

Now bring to mind a time when you felt genuinely happy. When you felt calm and centered. When your body felt grounded and stable. When your mind was clear. Think of a time in your life when you deliberately tended to your own inner environment to such a degree that nothing in the outer world could ruffle your feathers or cause you to lose your balance. Recall the feeling of alignment. Breathe into it and set the intention to reclaim it in this moment. You have the power and the ability to choose any emotional channel you desire, and you have the power and the ability to restore every part of yourself to the high vibration that reflects who you are at your core.

And with your next deep breath, begin to notice any impulses or ideas that come forth from the wiser, broader part of you as to what you could do, right in this moment, to fill your emotional cup even more. Trust whatever messages emerge, even if you don't recognize them consciously, knowing that you have within you all the wisdom you need to live in a perfect state of inner balance. And receive whatever asking you may hear about what the inner part of you needs in order to be filled to the brim—more time alone; more sleep; more laughter or more fun—knowing that life will present you with many opportunities for these requests to be fulfilled, and that you are deeply deserving of them. The more you do for yourself, the more you can do for others. This is one of nature's laws.

Take another few moments to enjoy the stillness and the peace you have created within the privacy of your own heart and mind. As you return your awareness to this time and place, know that you are bringing this expansive energy with you, and that it will infuse your every thought, word, and action for the rest of this day. And when you are ready, and taking as much time as you need, gently open your eyes.

In order to maintain the high-flying frequency you've chosen, you will probably have to become a little less interested in what other people are doing—and a whole lot less interested in what they are saying or thinking about you. You will have to become much less willing to indulge in self-criticism or self-pity. You'll have to stop engaging with and tolerating people and conversations that bring you down, and start walking away from potential arguments before they escalate. It will help if you consciously remember that those things occur on a frequency channel you are seeking to change, and that the remote control lives inside of you. The moment you find yourself in an experience that is out of sync with the quantum success you desire and deserve, imagine yourself getting up, walking across the room, and deliberately changing that channel. In other words, self-regulate.

Earlier this year, I started working with a personal trainer whom I hired primarily to support me in staying on track with regard to my diet, and after a few weeks of working together, I began to see a pattern within myself that brought me a lot of clarity. During the workweek or whenever I was traveling on business, I was very deliberate about my diet, and consistent about planning meals in advance. But anytime I went on vacation or spent weekend downtime hanging out with family, that discipline went right out the window. In my mind (or, more accurately, in my nervous system), I had made an association between family time and eating foods I normally stay away from, such as pasta, bread, and decadent, sugary coffee drinks. One day my trainer said matter-of-factly, "You know, Christy, as long as you associate free time with eating junk food, you'll never reach your goal." It was as if a light went on in my mind. She was absolutely right.

In thinking about how to unravel this non-serving association, I began to see that—as in all things—it truly was a matter of deciding which channel I was going to put the most focus on, and therefore make dominant within my own vibrational environment. Without even realizing it, I had allowed the easygoing, fun-loving, relaxing channel that I tune in to so easily when I'm with my family to bleed over into the more focused and deliberate-feeling channel I now wanted to tune to with regard to my fitness, and the two vibrations directly opposed one another. The solution was as simple as reminding myself of what I was choosing to create in the area of my diet *before* our weekend get-togethers, rather than using family time as a license to eat whatever and however much I wanted, only to beat myself up for it afterward, as had been my habit.

To become more deliberate about my weekend diet, I took some time in advance to think about where we were likely to eat, and to consider some healthy options that I would feel good about choosing at each meal. I also gave myself full permission to have one "cheat" meal per day (rather than a "cheat" weekend!). More importantly, I focused my daily meditations on the feelings that I want to experience in my body—those of lightness, sexiness, fitness, and ease—and bathed myself in these qualities on an energetic level. Once I changed the tone of the frequency of my internal thoughts and feelings, my preset family channel no longer dominated the airwaves, and my outer actions began to reflect that new momentum.

Unless we consciously declare within ourselves the channel we are committed to broadcasting on in each situation we encounter, it's very likely that our signal will entrain with whatever energy is dominant, even if this means sinking to the lowest common denominator. Whether it's the quality of food we're committed to eating or the number of sales we're committed to closing in a particular month, we have the ability to foster within us a vibration that will nurture that reality into being. If you want to be one of those people whom others describe as being in the zone or on a roll, you have to be willing to be the one who starts that ball rolling. You do this by deliberately tending to the inner environment of your most dominant thoughts and emotions, and providing that environment with the nourishment it needs to thrive. Conjure the feeling of success whenever the inspiration comes to you. Bask in the accomplishments of others, for what is possible for one is possible for all. Make it a point of noticing even the small things that are going well. Look for evidence of abundance all around you. Use everything you can find as a reason to feel good: this is how you create and sustain the energy of quantum success.

In the same way that different plants require different amounts of sun and water and different types of soil, the environment you prepare within your own energy field determines what will grow in the garden of your career. As you learn to master the art of tending to the field of your own energetic environment and modulating the degree of alignment you create before allowing momentum to build through your actions, you will find yourself engineering manifestations so brilliant and so perfect that they surprise even you.

Creating the Climate for Quantum Success: Putting It into Action

Begin by declaring yourself a deliberate creator of your life's experiences, rather than a creator by default, and make an internal resolution to prepare yourself internally before becoming engaged in any external interaction. Affirm to yourself that the outer world is a reflection of your inner world of imagination, thoughts, emotions, and beliefs, and that you and you alone are the source of these. In the same way a professional athlete prepares him- or herself—physically, mentally, and emotionally—before an important game, distinguish for yourself the rituals and daily practices that support you in performing at the top of your game, and which ones undermine your performance. Use the following technique in order to clarify this for yourself:

- Begin by making a list of the people in your career that you spend the most time with or the most time talking to on the phone, and notice which ones you consistently find yourself feeling negatively influenced by. Narrow it down to the top three whom you find most challenging, and then begin looking for patterns within yourself that make you less effective in maintaining the environment of your choice while in their presence. For example, if these are people that you have a habit of complaining about, or if you routinely feel sorry for yourself when the responsibilities of your job necessitate spending time with them, you are unwittingly practicing a vibration that invites and encourages them to offer the very behavior that you find most challenging. Be honest with yourself, and to the best of your ability, locate the thoughts, attitudes, expectations, and behaviors that you offer in relation to these folks that is inconsistent with the environment you want to maintain when with them.

- Next, identify at least three actions that you could take to increase your inner resilience and minimize their negative influence. You want to think in terms of things you can do in advance of seeing them that fill your emotional cup and strengthen the vibration you want to experience while with them—such as making a list of their positive aspects, or remembering times in the past when you worked well together—and you also want to think in terms of things you can do to periodically self-regulate while you are interfacing with them. For example, perhaps you would increase your odds of maintaining your desired frequency if you met via Skype rather than in person, or if you chose a meeting place other than the office. Once you start taking 100 percent responsibility for creating and maintaining your own emotional environment, you'll discover just how many options are available to help you do it.

- Lastly, make a commitment to regularly attend to the practices, rituals, and actions that support you in creating and maintaining a positive energy field—that contribute to your vitality or enhance your feeling of empowerment—knowing that these practices are the key to sustaining your chosen vibration.

7

PRUNING AS A CATALYST FOR GROWTH

"You never change things by fighting the existing reality. To change something, build a new model that makes the existing model obsolete."

—BUCKMINSTER FULLER

THE MOMENT YOU DECLARE A NEW INTENTION or create a new goal for yourself or your career, everything within you that has not yet come into alignment with that goal or desire will surface in the form of an obstacle to your success. These obstacles are actually vital to the creative process, because it is through living the contrast we don't want that we discover what we do.

Whether you realize it or not, you have actually been preparing for the career of your dreams all of the days of your life. This process of discovery began with the forming of questions early on that you didn't have ready answers to at the time—questions such as "What am I here to contribute?" or "How will I find work that fulfills me?" All of us—

consciously or unconsciously—have been asking these questions since childhood, in response to both the negative and positive experiences we witnessed in those around us.

Every time you saw a loved one come home exhausted at the end of the day or felt the stress in your household of not having enough money to make ends meet, you silently asked to be led to a vocation that provided energy, joy, and plenty of resources to live an abundant life. Every time you heard your mother or father judge someone who made a lot of money, you made a decision about yourself, and limitations began. And every time you saw someone living joyfully, doing something they loved, making a difference in the lives of others and attracting abundance along the way—whether it was someone who was known to you personally or not—this asking within you became even stronger as you intuitively understood that if success is possible for one, it's possible for all.

As you moved through time, you continued to gather life experiences that made these questions sharper and more specifically directed toward you, and often your asking far surpassed your knowing. If you're like most people, you've probably cycled through many periods in your life when you had no idea what kind of work you wanted to do, or, like me, when you questioned whether you were even born with a specific purpose at all. And then, inevitably, life calls each of us in a particular direction, and you found yourself becoming intrigued by some area of interest, or led by a series of events to explore a certain path. The discovery of your ideal career begins when an opportunity in the outer world speaks directly and powerfully to the questions and longings that have been stirring in your innermost self. It is a recognition not unlike love at first sight, and you may feel as though you have no choice but to move in the direction of this calling.

In my own life, it was the experience of being utterly unfulfilled—not only in my chosen career at the time, but also within myself—that led me on the path of self-discovery that would eventually evolve into the incredibly expansive and joyful work that I do today. As the old saying goes, when the student is ready, the teacher appears. Every one of your life experiences has been that teacher, and each has conspired to help you discover both the work you want to do in the world and the person you will need to become in order to do it. Contrast shows you clearly the parts of life you *don't* want to experience and the person you *don't* want to be. And from that clarity you are given both the opportunity and the imperative to make the internal shifts that will deliver you from who you've been to who you are becoming. Years ago, when I wanted to shift from being a person who struggled with going in and out of debt to a person who attracted, managed, saved, and wisely invested money, the change in my relationship with money began with that initial decision. If you were to observe my behaviors, you would see that I am a completely different person now in relation to money than I was in the past, but every change that I've manifested in terms of the actions I now take are the result of that initial burst of inner clarity, decision, and intention.

> Every one of your life experiences has been that teacher, and each has conspired to help you discover both the work you want to do in the world and the person you will need to become in order to do it.

From the moment I first invited you to begin envisioning your ideal, successful career, you have been in a process of gradually coming into internal alignment with the full realization of it. By now, I hope, you understand the importance of holding steady to the vision of what you truly want, even when evidence of that vision is not yet manifested in your present reality. With the new awareness that your emotions are like TV channels that you can tune to on purpose, you're likely becoming more practiced in the art of adjusting the frequency of your most common thoughts, moods, and feelings, and are perhaps starting to note the difference between words and actions that are inspired from a high vibration, and those that are offered from an internal state that is less-than-aligned. No matter where you are in this process of becoming—even if you have not yet seen any tangible evidence that your vision is coming to fruition, or if you perhaps fell short on an important project—you are nonetheless continuing to refine in greater detail the type of career success you desire to create. Whatever your particular situation, it's important to understand that as your vision continues to flesh out in full, living color, maintaining its forward momentum will call for a whole new level of energy mastery.

Perhaps you are the owner of your own business and have employees to manage, a payroll to make each month, and deadlines that you are accountable for meeting. Or maybe you are working within a corporate environment in which interpersonal skills are every bit as vital to your success as the credentials that landed you the job. Whatever the external state of your career at this moment—whether you'd describe it as thriving or faltering or even nonexistent—know that it is in a perpetual process of becoming even more. And in order to allow its evolution to continue unimpeded by resistance, you will have to overcome the very strong tendency to react to the day-to-day challenges you will inevitably face. The important thing to remember is that anytime something is drawn into your experience that opposes the experience you desire, you have a fundamental choice to make: you can focus on and complain about all that appears to be falling apart, or you can use that contrast to clarify exactly what you want to rebuild in its place. How you choose to relate to contrast when it shows up (and it will!) will determine whether you allow it to stop you in your tracks with anxiety or doubt, or propel you forward into the next level of success you are seeking. Understanding the Law of Detachment is key in making the most evolutionary choice.

The Law of Detachment

At first glance, a subject like detachment may seem out of place in a book about using the laws of deliberate creation to experience more joy and prosperity in your career, but once you understand the role that detachment plays in bringing any vision to fruition, you'll see how essential this principle is to sustaining forward motion.

Most of us were taught that if we want to make things happen in our lives, then we need to bring to bear the full force of our focus, conviction, and determination in a kind of "pedal to the metal" attitude. I, for one, was definitely raised with the belief that if I wanted to be successful, I needed to work hard and go after what I wanted with intensity. And this was the way I operated, with some measure of success, for the first decade of my adult life. But what I now understand is that, while applying effort is an important part of deliberate creating, most of us misunderstand which of our efforts actually yield the best results. Too often under the guise of manifesting our desires, we are actually attempting to control how, when, where, and with whom our desires will be fulfilled. And this not only gets us into trouble when things are unfolding differently than we've envisioned, but it also prevents us from seeing any possibilities that exist outside of our preconceived picture.

It's great to visualize, daydream, plan, and set goals, but at some point, we need to trust that these efforts have already been set into motion, and allow things to manifest in their own way and in their own time. Clinging too rigidly to a fixed idea of how things should be blinds us to the wisdom we can gain by appreciating them as they are, in the same way that trying too hard to force solutions to problems only creates more problems.

The universe holds a bird's-eye view of our lives and is more than capable of managing all the pieces of the puzzle comprising what each of us has come to conceive of as our ideal career expression. When we surrender our attachment to needing to know how, who, what, when, and where it will happen, and place our attention instead on simply aligning ourselves in heart and mind with the essence of our desire, the universe makes it happen for us. There is no pushing, shoving, manipulating, painstaking planning, or any of the other strategies that we've been taught to use to go after what we want. By surrendering the illusion that we are in control and simply allowing things to unfold, we summon the power of the Law of Detachment, which states that the fastest way to manifest any outcome is to relinquish our attachment to it.

I encourage you to redefine the concept of "effort," and to apply your effort in the ways that will give you the most bang for your buck: it takes more effort and mental focus to deliberately offer an energetic environment consistent with what you desire than to align by default with the influences of employees, bosses, clients, or coworkers—and this is an effort worth making. It takes the effort of dedicating yourself so fiercely to the vision of what has not yet manifested that you are willing to guard it from those who can only see what's already in front of them. But if it's something you truly care about—and I certainly hope that creating quantum success is something you care about deeply— then you really have no other choice but to maintain your belief in its eventual becoming.

Guarding Your Creations

Birds in the wild devote months of their lives to protecting their un- hatched eggs; most human parents would stop at almost nothing to keep their children safe from harm, and the rest of us would surely go out of our way to fight for a cause we believe in or to defend someone we care about whom we feel is being wronged. But how many of us take the same powerful energetic stand when it comes to guarding our own visions of wildly abundant success? The answer is, almost none, and there are plenty of ways we justify this. Some feel undeserving of receiving the level of success they dream of; others are still carrying around some ridiculous beliefs that keep them perpetually playing small—beliefs like "Life is about compromise," or "People won't like me if I'm too successful."

We don't defend our own creations with the same fierce protectiveness that we generate in almost every other area of our lives, and we need to! Just think how many times you have shared an idea about something you were inspired to create or pursue, only to have another person tear it apart and convince you of its failure. This happens daily in the lives of far too many of us, particularly in the workplace. In the name of explaining ourselves or maintaining rapport with those around us, we subject our precious visions to the chopping block of other people's opinions, thereby diminishing our own enthusiasm and flow of creativity. Thankfully, *we* are the ones who get to decide which aspects of our current circumstances to make relevant by feeding them with our attention, and which to make irrelevant by focusing our attention somewhere else.

> Identify things that you can focus on in the privacy of your own mind and imagination that light you up, inspire you, and support the kind of momentum you want to foster.

A big part of maintaining positive forward momentum—in your career or in any other aspect of your life—has to do with becoming more sensitive to the people, situations, and "facts" that it is best to withdraw your attention from, because focusing on them repeatedly takes the wind out of your sails. And hand in hand with this, it's also incredibly helpful to identify things that you *can* focus on in the privacy of your own mind and imagination that light you up, inspire you, and support the kind of momentum you want to foster. I call this cultivating "abundance consciousness," and while there are an infinite number of things you can do to keep your vibration flying high, integrating the principles that follow will give you a good place to start:

KEYS TO CULTIVATING ABUNDANCE CONSCIOUSNESS

1. *Consider the quality of the information you consistently expose yourself to.* Make a daily practice of reading, listening to, and meditating upon uplifting messages that encourage and are consistent with the vibration of abundance. If you have not done so already, visit www .ChristyWhitman.com, and register as a member of my thriving online community, so that you can begin to benefit immediately from the information, inspiration, and other free resources that I share on a weekly basis. Consider hiring one of my certified Law of Attraction coaches, all of whom are trained in these principles and skilled at holding space for abundance.

2. *Be mindful of your thoughts and words,* for these become your reality. Deliberately look for the most positive aspects you can find in each situation and person you encounter, and express your praise both silently and out loud. Release the low vibrations of criticism, jealousy, and resentment, knowing that lamenting the past will not deliver you to the future you desire.

3. *Seek out high-minded and like-minded others.* Surround yourself with spiritually aware and successful people who express qualities and character traits that you would like to emulate. What you consistently give your time and attention to, you eventually become.

4. *Give of your time, talents, money, and resources*—10 percent or more—to causes that call to you or inspire you, and extend generosity to those who contribute to you. Look for opportunities to help others get what they want; your assistance will come back to you tenfold. The

practice of tithing is grounded in the universal principle that you must give in order to receive, and is one of the greatest secrets to generating wealth.

5. *Think, walk, stand, speak, and behave as though you already are the person you desire to become.* Pay attention to your posture, dress in a manner that reflects your definition of success, and invest time and resources in caring for your appearance. Act the part, as if you are the actor or actress cast in a starring role—because you are.

6. *Clarify your desired outcome* in advance of each important event or interaction, and visualize it as having already unfolded brilliantly.

7. *Joyfully expect that good and wonderful things are in the process of flowing into your life right now.* Look for these blessings, notice them, and appreciate them—either by recording them in a journal or by giving thanks for them daily. The more you appreciate the positive things, the more positive things you will have to appreciate.

True leadership is not determined by who can speak the loudest, or even by who is the most qualified or has the best ideas. We are compelled to follow those who are high-minded, abundant, and so in alignment with their own cause that they no longer feel the need to convince others of its validity. I heard once that the difference between a good leader and an extraordinary leader is that when a good leader uses words to motivate her team, the team applauds and says, "Good speech." But when an extraordinary leader communicates, her team responds with a resounding, "Let's march!" Remember that you are communicating with everything and everyone around you and with the universe at large every moment of every day by virtue of the energetic signal you are sending out, and the quality and tone of that communication is being received by all and returned in kind.

There is no more important time to keep your energetic environment deliberate and strong than when you are entering into an outer environment of potential opposition. Think of the energetic environment you carry around with you as a surgical room that for the safety of the patient must be kept impeccably clean. In the same way a surgeon would not permit even one potential contaminant to enter the sterile room, you want to become vigilant about and intolerant of even seemingly innocent gossip, negative observations, and complaints. They may appear casual, but they are not. And when what you perceive as the negativity of others triggers a less-than-good feeling within you, just know that you will likely be tempted to hold them responsible for how you feel and for "knocking you off your game"—but in truth, you are the only one who has the power to affect your vibration, for the good and for the bad. When you find yourself feeling frustrated, hurt, or annoyed in response to another person's behavior, recognize this as simply an indication that there is a thought, belief, or perspective within you that is not in alignment with your vision and therefore needs to be shifted, and—using the processes you've learned throughout this book—go about the business of shifting it. The faster you do this—and ideally before you vocalize your grievance to anyone else—the less negative momentum you will create.

Every thought we think creates something, and it does so even faster when we focus those thoughts into words. The degree of sensitivity I am inviting you to develop is one in which you ask yourself, before uttering any word or even making a simple gesture, "In which direction is this action leading me, and do I really want to arrive at that destination?" It takes a tremendous amount of discipline not to fire back at someone or something that you perceive as threatening the success of a creation that you care about, and this is why I recommend that you prepare your environment in advance. Ideally, so much of your attention will be focused on looking everywhere in your environment for evidence of quantum success that the voice of opposition can't be heard over the beautiful symphony you are creating in your own head.

To create a reality beyond what you formerly thought possible, you must continuously invite new energy into your life. Seek out people who are already doing in the world something similar to what you want to do, who are already demonstrating quantum success in their own way, and consciously align yourself with their energy. You can join Facebook groups made up of those who are engaged in work that is similar or related to what you want to do. You can check out business networking groups to meet new people who have no reference point for what type of work you've done in the past, and relate to you only in terms of the career you are in the process of moving into. You can reconnect with those from your past whom you've admired or regard as being good at what they do, and ask them to share their secrets to success.

Whenever you catch yourself saying things like "She was really a good communicator," or "That place had a great vibe," take it as a signal to stop and really pay attention. So often, these are a sign, a clue, a whisper from the universe urging you to take a step in a particular direction. Once you become open to actively receiving them, you'll be amazed at how one search leads you to the next; and as you research those who are in a career that you envision for yourself, or making the kind of impact that you'd like to make, you can gain inspiration and ideas from finding out about the events that led them to that path. John Assaraf, a bestselling author, one of the leading behavioral and mind-set experts in the world, and one of the people I admire the most in the field of personal development, recently appeared as a guest on my weekly *Quantum Success* webcast, and spoke candidly about the difficulties he encountered growing up, and how finding a mentor radically altered what might have been a very negative life trajectory.

John shared that, as a teen, he struggled in school and faced violence at home, and eventually—after finding acceptance with a rough crowd of boys who were always getting into trouble—began getting into fistfights daily and eliciting even more punishment from his hardworking but unrelenting father. By the time he was nineteen, John's teachers and parents all believed that it was only a matter of time before he wound up in jail or the morgue. And then, one day while on a train from Montreal to Toronto, he met a man named Alan Brown, who believed in John more than he believed in himself, and who would ultimately become John's mentor and forever change the course of his life.

Alan succeeded in capturing John's attention with a single question: "What do you want to trade your life for?" When John asked him to clarify what he meant, Alan said, "Well, every day when you wake up, you are trading your life for what it is that you do. You're trading your life for whatever it is you're trying to accomplish. You're trading your life for hanging around the people you're hanging around with. You're trading your life during that day or that moment or that hour." These words sparked a realization within John that he had never before considered. For the first time, he began evaluating his choices and asking himself if they were worth trading his life for.

John then recalled another piece of advice he'd learned from his mentor, related specifically to the practice of goal-setting, which is completely in line with my philosophy and with everything I've been sharing with you throughout this book. "People who live average lives look at their current situations, knowledge, skills, abilities, resources, money, friends, etcetera, and then choose the goals that they think they could achieve with those resources—and this," John explained—and I agree completely—"is backwards." First we need to determine what it is we want to achieve, and *then* figure out what knowledge, resources, and tools we'll need to make those goals and dreams a reality.

Just think of the wealth of collective resources that you have access to right now. No matter what goal you want to accomplish or what field you want to excel in, there are people who have succeeded in that very endeavor, who have mastered that skill, and who have gained tremendous wisdom as a result of all they've learned in the process. And, like John's mentor Alan, those who have already accomplished the level of mastery you are striving for are often more than happy to share their wisdom with those who are eager to receive it. There are potential mentors all around you; you just need to be clear about what type of guidance would best serve you, and be open to recognizing those who have those gifts to give.

When seeking out a mentor, the most crucial factor you are looking for is inspiration. What about this person inspires you? What page from the playbook of their life could you try out for yourself? When you encounter someone, even a stranger, who is demonstrating a quality that you find attractive or a feature about which you're curious—maybe it's the way they handled themselves in a meeting, or a particular type of planner they are using to organize their time efficiently—be bold and strike up a conversation. How did they first develop this habit? What practices or disciplines support them in their ongoing success? What recommendations, if any, might they have for you? If you find it hard to imagine yourself being so forthright, think for a moment about how you would feel if a stranger asked you about something that you consider to be a personal asset or strength. Wouldn't you feel honored that they had noticed, and at least somewhat inclined to engage?

One of the secrets to my success is that I have continually had coaches or mentors by my side who have helped me to see beyond current obstacles and limitations, and realign myself in times when I've lost sight of my vision. We all have a tendency to fall into tunnel vision; a mentor or coach supports us in having total vision. A mentor is someone who leads by example, and someone through whom we can see and connect with our own latent potential. Mary Morrissey is such a person for me. She demonstrates the type of successful woman, wife, and mother that I continually strive to be, and inspires me to keep reaching for more.

When your eyes are open to it, you will begin to see that the world around you is literally teeming with living, breathing examples of those who have created their own version of quantum success and would love nothing more than to help you find your way. Tune your attention to these opportunities, practice being open to receive, and give yourself permission to act upon the impulses that occur. In surrounding yourself with inspiring people, you will find yourself becoming more inspired without even trying. "Becoming the change" you want to create in the area of your career means just that—you must be it, step into it, and embody it within yourself, long before evidence in the outer world has gathered to affirm it. This is the real definition of what it means to be "self-made." And whether you are making yourself in the image of success or in the image of failure, you are the one who is doing it.

The Law of Polarity: Creating in the Presence of Contrast

As a result of everything we've explored throughout this book, you now know that you are the creator of the career experience that you are now living—good, bad, or ugly—and that you are *not* a victim of circumstance. Of course, this realization cuts both ways. Understanding that you are actually drawing to yourself the circumstances and events that enter your life is an incredible, empowering feeling when things are going well and your intended results are unfolding nicely. And you deserve to celebrate and acknowledge these successes as they unfold, because you were the author and the creator of those experiences.

It's when things are not working out as planned or moving forward as easily as we would like that the knowledge that we created those circumstances doesn't feel so great. In fact, understanding that we are the creators of whatever reality we are currently living can greatly compound the discomfort we feel when our career expression is not in the condition we'd like it to be. And yet, this contrast between the reality we want to live and the reality we are currently living is an essential part of the creative process, because we are never more acutely aware of what we really want than when we are faced with its opposite.

The Law of Polarity is based on the understanding that human life exists along a broad spectrum of possibilities ranging from what each of us would consider to be extremely positive and desirable to what we would define as negative or unwanted. Regardless of where you find yourself along this continuum of experience, you always have the potential to experience its polar opposite. Just think about it: it's in those moments when you finally reach a breaking point, when you've had all you can take of an unworkable situation, that real determination is born and change can begin. And it's when the discomfort becomes so great that you can no longer deny that you're not happy where you are that you become willing to face the unknown and take the next steps. The Law of Polarity is integral in every experience and every act of creation. You could not know light were it not for the contrast of darkness; you would never recognize the satisfaction of being full unless you had experienced hunger; and you could not appreciate the victory of having achieved something unless you had first experienced the pain of wanting it. We live in a universe of contrasting values, and it takes one extreme to know the other.

Whether it shows up as something mildly irritating or majorly troubling, and whether we experience it as the absence of something wanted or the presence of something unwanted, contrast serves a very specific purpose. It draws our attention to a discord that exists between our inner desire and our outer reality, and this discord creates a point of tension that we register in our bodies and minds as a feeling of discontent, disappointment, impatience, and a lot of other emotions we typically label as negative. But it's from this very point of tension that an intention is born, and with a clarity that can only arise from raw, unfiltered feeling, a powerful signal is transmitted instantaneously through every fiber of our being: *I want something different! I want something* more!!

In the same way that necessity is the mother of all invention, the experience of not having what we want is the driving force behind all change. Abusive bosses, catty coworkers, production delays . . . all of these expressions of contrast are a necessary part of life, because there can be no expansion without the realization that we'd like some aspect of our lives to improve. When there is discord between our inner desire and any outer condition, that discord will eventually create a tipping point. We reach a state mentally, emotionally, and energetically in which we simply "can't take it anymore," and a powerful decision rises up within us to begin bridging the gap between what we have and what we want. And we bridge this gap by, as quickly as we can, taking our focus off the contrast that inspired our newfound clarity and placing it on the reality we are now being called toward, and what it will feel like once we've achieved it. If you can learn to appreciate—to savor, even—the process of this becoming; if you can delight in each new desire for something more that bursts forth from within you, trusting that in the same way that a seed grows silently underground before any evidence of its growth becomes visible, the dreams of your heart are making their way into the manifested, tangible world, you will become a much more cooperative component of this natural unfolding.

When we consider the biological growth of a plant or the development of a human being, we respect this natural cycle of growth, and the last thing we'd want to do is interrupt the process by becoming impatient. We don't dig up the apple seed the day after it's been planted, expecting to eat an apple for lunch, and we'd never want to give birth to a baby the day after becoming pregnant! Instead, we tend to these creations at each phase of their growth, trusting that all things will ripen in their own time. And yet, when it comes to the unfolding of our own career expression—and the freedom, fulfillment, and financial abundance we associate with it—we rarely extend this same understanding or patience.

So often, our aspirations of great career achievement are thwarted by impatience, or by an expectation of overnight success—and I certainly understand this perception. From the outside looking in, as you begin to contemplate or reconsider what kind of work would provide the greatest soul satisfaction for you and value to others, it's easy to convince yourself that with enough education, planning, money, or support, you could go directly from point A to point Z. But not only is it unrealistic to expect to achieve instantaneous results straight out of the gate, it's not even desirable. Why? Because the insights you will gain on the journey of designing your ideal career will naturally cause your vision to evolve. Today, my coaching academy is a thriving worldwide enterprise—metaphorically speaking, a huge, fruit-laden tree that supports all of those who in some way support me—but it started out as a tiny sprout that I nourished one day at a time, one decision at a time, and one client at a time.

Once we become aware of an unwanted reality or a not-yet-manifested desire, most of us would, if we could, simply snap our fingers and turn it all around on a dime. And yet if we had the power to do this, we would actually be depriving ourselves of the most valuable part of the manifestation process, which is the shift we are being called to bring about in the inner realm of our beliefs, moods, perceptions, and patterns of thought and behavior that are no longer in alignment with who we are at our core, or with who we desire to become. Being a deliberate creator means consciously practicing within ourselves the vibration of what is wanted, rather than allowing our vibration to become entrained by whatever may be happening around us.

It's easy to simply sit back, observe, and respond positively to positive conditions; but in times of contrast, our ability to maintain our internal environment and remain on our chosen channel regardless of what anyone else is choosing is strengthened. And when you stop to think about it, true satisfaction never comes about when someone else paves our road to success, but only as a result of feeling our own way through the obstacles that present themselves along our path. It's who we become inside as we make the decision not to allow circumstances to impede the unfolding of our vision that makes us truly feel proud of ourselves at the end of the day.

Contrast compels us to look beyond what is currently playing out around us; to reconstitute within ourselves the vibrational and emotional essence of what is desired; and to bring ourselves back into alignment with it. In the metaphoric garden that is our career, there are times when it's in the best interest of our unfolding vision to devote more energy, care, and maintenance to a certain creation, and other times when the contrast we are experiencing is because some aspect of our career is in need of healthy pruning.

Changing Course and Cutting Back

It may seem counterintuitive, but the act of weeding out people, projects, and practices that have grown stagnant or are no longer effective actually serves as a catalyst for new growth—like upgrading an old computer operating system that, while familiar, is holding us back from a whole new level of productivity. Releasing that which no longer fits is a vital part of attracting a more perfect fit—yet most of us resist this natural process. We view letting go as a loss, so we cling to the old rather than release it to embrace the new. We hold on to old duties rather than delegate them, because we are afraid to let go of the reins. We stay in careers that no longer fulfill us because we are afraid of letting go. And fear of letting go is certainly at play when we stay at jobs that limit us or don't compensate us for the value that we bring.

Just as it's important to continue to expand your vision of your ideal career, it's also essential to pay attention to signs that your professional growth is being hindered by investing energy in things that no longer yield a return. If, out of fear of "rocking the boat," we allow ourselves to linger too long in a job that is no longer stimulating or supporting our expansion, we may find ourselves fearfully saying no instead of boldly saying yes when a big opportunity comes our way.

When I first began doing one-on-one coaching with Evelyn, who is now my dear friend and amazing colleague, she was the owner of two busy tanning salons, which she operated and managed full-time. As both a fan of spray tans and a natural at customer service, Evelyn liked her job and loved serving her clients; but with two locations and employees to oversee at opposite ends of town, along with two young children at home, she often felt frazzled and like she was always on the run. On a call early in our coaching relationship, Evelyn shared that she would enjoy having the opportunity to spend more time with each client, and to perhaps expand the services she offered to include alternative modalities such as energy work to help balance and inspire her clients to embody the best version of themselves, but she was so busy with the daily operations of both salons that she simply didn't have the time.

During the course of our work together, Evelyn came to appreciate the contrast of her overbooked life as providing valuable clarity into the type of career she desired to transition into: while the challenge of managing two startup salons had initially been fun and exciting, and while she believed in the product she offered, she now desired to find work that served a greater purpose. She wanted to wake up each day feeling passionate about the contribution her work enabled her to make to others, and she also wanted a career that offered the opportunity to earn an unlimited amount of money while working fewer hours and minimizing her daily commute. Eventually, Evelyn decided that she wanted to become certified as a life coach, and that in order to move forward toward this dream, she would need to sell her interest in her tanning salons and bring that chapter of her professional life to a close. The way her life and her work schedule were set up, she simply couldn't see a way to continue working full-time and simultaneously pursue a completely different career. She had to choose between holding on to the status quo, and letting it fall away in favor of allowing in something new.

As a result of applying the universal laws and principles that I've shared throughout this book, Evelyn was able to attract the perfect buyer for her business, and the sale left her with both the financial resources and the freedom to pursue her coaching business full-time, and to eventually design and facilitate remarkable advanced energy courses that have helped hundreds of people and that fill her soul with purpose. Evelyn is a beautiful example of the power of letting go of a career expression that she'd outgrown in order to make space for her heart's desire to bloom. She recognized the opportunity when it presented itself, took the leap, and has never looked back. Now a full-time coach and coach trainer, Evelyn is engaged in work that she is passionate about and feels called to do, and is making more money than her salon business ever yielded, or that she even thought was possible for herself.

Everything in life is always in a process of becoming more—and your career is no different—so it's necessary to periodically reevaluate what you're doing and how, so that you can cut back on the products, services, and activities that aren't truly essential to your bottom line. For example, when I first left the corporate world to start my coaching practice, I began leading a free monthly call that was responsible for attracting almost 100 percent of my client base. Over time, however, that referral base has continued to grow. One inspired idea at a time, I have expanded my business model from providing only one-on-one coaching to facilitating group coaching sessions each month, to eventually teaching weekend retreats, developing a year-long coaching certification program, and making a portion of the principles and practices on which my work is founded available via online courses that participants can complete at their own pace and in the privacy of their own homes. At each developmental stage, I reevaluated the results I was achieving and the number of people I was able to reach. One day as I was looking over a search-engine optimization report generated by my Web team, I saw that my *Quantum Success Shows*, which are filmed in-studio and air each week, were getting thousands of views on YouTube, and I realized this was a far more effective means of introducing people to my work than leading that free monthly call.

In light of the fact that I now had hundreds of referral sources and my business had expanded to the point that I only had time to coach a handful of clients one-on-one, I decided that continuing to lead the free monthly call was no longer a good use of my time, even though I had always done it. By taking the time to reevaluate this action in the context of my evolving values and priorities, it was easy to see that it no longer made sense. In this case, by pruning back the old, I made space for new, life-giving projects and pursuits.

Becoming an Essentialist

I first ran across the word *essentialist* one day while doing a Google search on the Internet. The word intrigued me, so I gave myself permission to take a short side trip in order to find out more. That's when I discovered the work of Greg McKeown, author of the book *Essentialism: The Disciplined Pursuit of Less*.[14] The book's subtitle caught my eye—I am, after all, the author of a book entitled *The Art of Having It All!* On the surface, the philosophies of these two works may appear to be diametrically opposed; but after delving into McKeown's thesis, I realized how similar his message is to my own.

Reading on, I learned that an *essentialist* is the term Greg uses to describe someone who no longer allows him- or herself to "get caught up in that furor of the frenzied, frenetic nonsense," and pursues instead only those things that really matter most. When he went on to explain that "the way of the Essentialist means living by design, not by default," I knew that my Internet search had led me to another kindred spirit—as they so often do! Making the deliberate decision to prune, to cut back on or cut out entirely those activities that aren't truly vital to fulfilling our visions of quantum success, is an act of essentialism. By continually clarifying and refining what's deeply important, we can become more selective in what we choose to grow in that proverbial garden that is our career. And in deliberately choosing not to spread ourselves too thin, we have more love, energy, and intention to apply toward the projects that really matter, and we reap a more bountiful and rewarding crop.

Everything we see and focus upon we create an energetic relationship with, and relationships require time and attention to maintain. So from an energetic perspective, the less scattered our focus, the more time and attention we will have to devote to the people, projects, and things that are truly important. In the course of my work, people often ask me why they are having a hard time manifesting the success they desire, and the first thing I have them look at is to what, where, and to how many people and projects they are directing their energy and attention. The vast majority of the time, when people feel stuck or unable to bring about the changes they desire, it's because they are devoting too much of their attention to things that they either don't enjoy or that don't contribute meaningfully to the fulfillment of their vision. Of course, necessities—such as shopping, running errands, and cooking—are all a part of life; but if you perform these activities begrudgingly, you are introducing a lot of resistance into your vibration that will make you less focused and effective when doing the things you love or that really matter. There are always far more alternatives and solutions than we allow ourselves to see, and there is nothing that blinds us to those solutions more than the belief that we must do everything ourselves. By focusing on what we love and delegating what we don't, we multiply our power of focus many times over.

My dear friend J.J. Virgin, who is a wildly successful nutritional and fitness expert and a multiple *New York Times* best-selling author, once shared with me that when she was in college, she would hire people to run errands and do her grocery shopping so that she could focus completely on school and work. J.J. understood that we only have a certain amount of time and energy, and that it was in her best interest to periodically reevaluate how she was spending both and to prune away the activities that don't yield a big reward. She still operates under this principle today when managing her multi-million-dollar business.

What follows is a checklist that can help you determine which of your "crops" are actively contributing to the fulfillment of your vision—and are therefore deserving of your time and attention—and which are extraneous or no longer vital to your success. Read and answer each question in relation to your current career in order to gain a better understanding of which aspects of it are providing value to you and are therefore worth rededicating yourself to, and which ones you are less than satisfied with and might choose to revise or cut back:

CAREER ALIGNMENT CHECKLIST

• *On my best of days, do I genuinely enjoy what I do?* We all have days when we feel out of sorts, so for this question, bring to mind your very best of days. Are you excited to get up and go? Do ideas and solutions come easily? Do you feel efficient and in the flow? If the majority of your time spent on the job is not enjoyable, this may be a sign that there is a more perfect career fit for you than the one you're currently in.

• *Do I feel effective at my job? Are my clients or customers satisfied with the results I produce?* While earning a paycheck is one important way we are compensated for the energy we give out, we receive tremendous personal benefit when we take pride in our accomplishments.

• *Do I feel compensated for the products or services that I provide?* And if the "input" currently exceeds the "output," what could you adjust or recalibrate in order to create more balance?

• *In general, does my current career path light me up and contribute to my vitality, or do I view it as a waste of energy or a drain of my life force?* Reflect on the effect your work has on the quality of your vibration, and on what changes you could make to keep your vibration high.

• *Do I feel like I am making a difference or fulfilling my purpose?* If large chunks of your time are spent doing things that are menial or feel unimportant, this may be the result of a lack of prioritization. Rather than struggling to get too many things done, look to see what changes you could make to ensure that you're staying focused on what's most important.

Important vs. Urgent

Oftentimes the greatest contributor to career dissatisfaction—and the hidden reason you might have answered in the negative to one or more of the questions above—is not related to *what* we are doing, but to *how* we are approaching what we do. So many of us have fallen into the habit of spending hours each day trying to get caught up on e-mails or allowing each phone call or coworker who pops into our office to interrupt a meaningful train of thought. In the short term, falling prey to these types of distraction may seem insignificant, but if we lose sight of what's truly important—making a difference, providing satisfaction to those we serve, being compensated (monetarily and otherwise) for our skills and talents, the enjoyment we feel as we allow ourselves to generously express those talents—it's easy to lose touch with the deeper *why* that drew us to our careers in the first place, and our satisfaction goes out the window. It's the *why* that fuels us with energy and ingenuity and inspiration, but we have to actively keep this *why* alive in our awareness, or it will get lost in a cloud of busy-ness.

Few of us were taught effective time-management, and yet this is precisely the skill that we need to develop in order to stay connected with and inspired by the parts of our jobs that we truly do love. As Dwight Eisenhower said, "What is important is seldom urgent and what is urgent is seldom important." Given that we now live in a world where we are inundated by cell phone chimes, buzzers, and a myriad of other attention-seeking devices, it's more essential than ever to be able to distinguish the difference between the two—and to have a game plan for giving our attention to the highest priority.

Years ago, I learned about a simple technique used by Charles Schwab—the founder of the world's largest brokerage house, which now has 235 branch offices worldwide—to ensure he was giving his attention to what was most important. At the end of each day, he would create a list of things that he wanted to accomplish the following day relevant to whatever were his current goals. But unlike the looming to-do lists that most of us now haul around day after day, this list was to contain only the six most important things to be completed the following day. Each morning, Schwab would start his day by working on the first item on that list, and would not move on until it was completed.

This one habit, when applied daily, leads to at least two very significant accomplishments. First, it provides a respite from the countless distractions that vie for our attention from the moment we sit down at the desk and allows our minds to focus single-pointedly on exactly what we'll work on first—and what comes after that, and what comes after that. But second, and far more beneficial, is that by deliberately tending to what is important instead of habitually reacting to what is urgent, we train ourselves in the art of prioritizing. And when an interruption comes our way, as it inevitably will, we can quickly discern whether it's something worthy of our immediate attention, whether we are best served by delaying it, or whether to dismiss it altogether. It may seem trivial, but there is no more important skill to develop than this type of discernment. And the more success you create, the more essential it will become.

I often tease my mentoring clients that once they begin to understand and really apply the universal laws that we've been exploring throughout this book—and especially when they master the Law of Sufficiency and Abundance—they are going to have a lot more opportunities and options coming their way than ever before. The key to staying focused on what really matters is to be really clear about your vision and to resist the temptation to deviate from it.

I can tell you from my own experience that the more choices you have—the more opportunities that open up for you; the more affiliations you have; the more effective you become at your chosen career or trade—the more people will be clamoring for your attention, and without the ability to prioritize them based on your ever-changing values and desires, the scenario of having too many choices can be just as difficult as feeling as though you have none. As long as our hearts are beating, we will all continue to generate new desires and intentions—and old priorities will by necessity fall by the wayside as new ones come into view. Because we live in an abundant universe, there will always, always be more. Even if you already have an abundance of love, success, joy, freedom . . . there is *always* more for you to experience, for the simple reason that this universe never ends.

Pruning as a Catalyst for Growth: Putting It into Action

Begin by bringing to mind a specific situation in the area of your career that you'd like to be different, or that you have actively been working to change. As you bring to mind the situation as it currently exists, reflect on these things specifically:

- *Are there certain elements of this role that I feel I've outgrown, or am less passionate about than I used to be?*

- *Are there meetings, affiliations, or other commitments that I regularly give my time and energy to that would be better invested in other ways?* What aspects of your business or career are in need of pruning? Think in terms of your weekly schedule as well as monthly and annual commitments.

- *What outdated systems or methods do I currently use, and what benefits might I receive by revamping these?* What resources could you draw from to support you in upgrading this aspect of your business? Who might you ask to serve as a mentor for you in this area?

Next, as you feel the point of tension created by the contrast between how this situation is currently playing out and how you would like it to be, remind yourself that from contrast, clarity always follows, and that you have the power to decide on which end of this spectrum you will place your focus. Reflecting again on this same situation, answer the following questions:

- *What do I want?*

- *Why do I want it?*

- *How will I feel having it?*

- *What do I need to release in order to have it?*

- *Who do I need to become to be a vibrational match to it?*

- *What are the six most important things for me to do tomorrow (and the next day, and the day after that) to bring myself closer to this goal?*

CONCLUSION

ENDING A BOOK ABOUT CREATING QUANTUM SUCCESS is not an easy task, because quantum success is not something that one creates from simply reading a book and doing the exercises. It is the result of embracing a whole new paradigm of life and way of living. In many ways, it is more a process of unlearning the false premises that most people are steeped in because they don't yet know there are other options, and of allowing our choices to be guided by entirely different points of reference. To create the true, unlimited success and happiness you desire, you will need to stop thinking of yourself—your credentials, your past experiences, and what you are able to accomplish through applying mental and physical force alone—as the source that generates the abundance in your life. You are not the source of your abundance, but rather a conduit through which abundance flows, and the only limitation to how much you can receive is how much you can learn to allow.

You did not take birth in this time and space to waste your life proving that you are worthy or lovable or capable. You are not here to prove that you can overcome the adversity of your past, or to make anyone else wrong for the role they played in it. You did not incarnate in a physical body for the purpose of getting others to like you, to approve of you, or to agree with you, and it is not your job to mold yourself to meet anyone else's expectations. If you haven't done so already, I invite you to give yourself the tremendous gift of withdrawing your energy and attention from any and all of those pursuits, right now, because they are a waste of this precious life experience.

You are a part of the unbounded stream of energy that sources everything, and you have chosen to be here, in a material body that is bound by time, in order to make manifest the desires that you hold dear in your heart. The opportunity of this lifetime—and the promise of continually seeking a career expression that remains up to speed with your evolving desires—is to discover who you are and what you enjoy. Your career expression will inevitably serve many others, but you are its primary beneficiary.

> The opportunity of this lifetime—and the promise of continually seeking a career expression that remains up to speed with your evolving desires—is to discover who you are and what you enjoy.

You are the true authority: the author of your own life. You have the freedom, the power, and the right to design and redesign a career that inspires you completely, and that calls you to show up in each situation as the very best version of you that you are capable in any moment of being. In the act of delivering your unique gifts to the world, you magnetize success not only in business, but in every aspect of your life.

The processes I've outlined throughout this book are designed to guide you to the most sublime experience of all—that of allowing the energy of life to flow through you, and to feel life itself living *as* you.

And, as we've explored, the way to create this experience, over and over—in your career and in every other area of your life—is to allow yourself to dream your next level of success; to establish an energetic connection with that dream by clarifying, visualizing, and *feeling* your vision as if it's already a reality; and to apply, moment by moment, the art and practice of bringing your thoughts, perceptions, moods, attitudes, and expectations into alignment with that vision. When you are tempted to allow the circumstances of your already-manifested reality to lure you off track, and you will be, remind yourself that your only job is to align your energy with what you want, rather than what you've got. When you are in energetic resonance with your desire, and stabilized in that frequency, momentum will ensue, and you'll be inspired to delicious ideas and to rewarding courses of action.

Creating quantum success in your career is a process of continually clarifying what else you desire to experience in the course of sharing your unique talents, perspectives, and skills with the world, and of continuing to apply the steps above at each stage of your personal and professional evolution. And it's essential to realize that, because you do not have the full picture of all that is possible for you at any given moment in time, you can only see a small fraction of the success that is actually available to you.

For example, as of this moment, your vision of your ideal career may only have evolved as far as a desire to start your own business. But once that manifestation occurs, your vision will continue to expand: perhaps owning your own business will cause within you a desire to work less, or to focus the services you offer to a more specialized niche of people. Even as you are engaged in your career in its current form, you can continue to find resonance with the next evolution of it, and the next one after that. Once you learn how to continually align your energy with each new expression you are reaching for, there is no end to the level of fulfillment you can create.

When you are in energetic resonance with your desire, and stabilized in that frequency, momentum will ensue, and you'll be inspired to delicious ideas and to rewarding courses of action.

The most exciting part of creation is *not* the getting. It's the *becoming*. It's in the process of making the adjustments to become an energetic match to your ever-evolving desires that you realize that nothing outside yourself is the source of your fulfillment. You are the source of your own fulfillment. The essence of all that you seek exists within you in seed form: yours to nourish and bring to life, seed after beautiful seed. Ultimately, your career path is a catalyst to realizing and expressing your full potential. You may think that the new title, improved status, or increase in income is what you are after—and, of course, to some extent, it is—but as a spiritual being, what you are truly seeking is the experience of growth and expansion that you will realize as you become a vibrational match to each of your evolving desires. You are seeking the joy and fulfillment of making your love visible and of finding the avenues of creative expression that are the perfect fit for you. This is how your career continues to expand, and it's also how your career expands you. And as far as I can tell, this process of expansion never ends.

ACKNOWLEDGMENTS

To my incredible Dream Team, without whom I would not be able to do the work I do: Danielle Dorman, Tammy Lawman, Evelyn Apostolou, Theresa Hoermann, Tabitha Hamilton, Beth Myers, Nada Howarth, Julie Kleinhans, and Rachel Christie. Know that I hold the deepest gratitude and love for each one of you.

And to my incredible clients, who allow me to do the work I LOVE. Thank you!

ENDNOTES

1   Dr. Martin Luther King Jr., "Commemoration of the 100-Year Anniversary of the Preliminary Emancipation Proclamation by Dr. Martin Luther King Jr., delivered at the Park-Sheraton Hotel in New York City," September 12, 1962, https://www.pbs.org/newshour/nation/new-speech-by-martin-luther-king-jr-surfaces.

2   Peter Drucker, *The Practice of Management* (New York: Harper, 1954).

3   Deepak Chopra, *Reinventing the Body, Resurrecting the Soul* (New York: Harmony, reprint edition, October 2010).

4   Karen Barad, *Meeting the Universe Halfway* (Durham, NC: Duke University Press, 2007).

5   Masaru Emoto, *The Hidden Messages in Water* (New York: Atria, September 2005).

6   Werner Heisenberg, *The Physical Principles of the Quantum Theory* (Mineola, NY: Dover Publications, June 1949).

7   Richard Panek, *The 4 Percent Universe* (New York: Mariner Books, October 2011).

8   Eckhart Tolle, *The Power of Now* (Vancouver: Namaste Publishing, 1997).

9   David Hawkins, *Power vs. Force* (Carlsbad, CA: Hay House Publishing, 2014).

10   Esther Hicks and Jerry Hicks, *Ask and It Is Given* (Carlsbad, CA: Hay House Publishing, 2004).

11   Ellen DeGeneres, *Seriously . . . I'm Kidding* (New York: Grand Central Publishing, 2011).

12   Esther Hicks and Jerry Hicks, "The Art of Allowing Workshop," delivered in San Diego, CA, August 2001.

13   T. Harv Eker, *Secrets of the Millionaire Mind* (New York: Harper-Business, February 2005).

14   Greg McKeown, *Essentialism: The Disciplined Pursuit of Less* (New York: Crown Business, April 2014).

ABOUT THE AUTHOR

Christy Whitman is a transformational leader, a Master Certified Coach, the *New York Times* bestselling author of *The Art of Having It All,* and coauthor of the bestselling *Taming Your Alpha Bitch.* She has appeared on the *Today* show and *The Morning Show,* and her work has been featured in *People, Seventeen, Woman's Day, Hollywood Life,* and *Teen Vogue,* among other publications. As the CEO and founder of the Quantum Success Coaching Academy, a twelve-month Law of Attraction coaching certification program, Christy has helped thousands of people worldwide to achieve their goals through her empowerment seminars, speeches, coaching sessions, and products. She currently lives in Scottsdare, Arizona, with her husband and their two boys.